A Must Read For All Seekers Of Truth
25 Years Of Guru Sannidhi

THE STORY OF MY SPIRITUAL JOURNEY

Rakesh K. Mittal

STERLING PAPERBACKS
An imprint of
Sterling Publishers (P) Ltd.
Regd. Office: A1/256 Safdarjung Enclave,
New Delhi-110029. CIN: U22110DL1964PTC211907
Tel: 26387070, 26386209; Fax: 91-11-26383788
E-mail: mail@sterlingpublishers.com
www.sterlingpublishers.com

The Story of My Spiritual Journey
© 2016, Rakesh K. Mittal
ISBN 978 81 207 9499 3

All rights are reserved.
No part of this publication may be reproduced, stored in a retrieval system or transmitted, in any form or by any means, mechanical, photocopying, recording or otherwise, without prior written permission of the original publisher.

Printed in India

Printed and Published by Sterling Publishers Pvt. Ltd.,
Plot No. 13, Ecotech-III, Greater Noida - 201306,
Uttar Pradesh, India

Gratitude

- My first gratitude for this book is for Poojya Swami Bhoomananda Tirtha, who gave me the permission as well as inspiration for writing the book. He also gave me valuable guidance for the contents of the book, in order to make it useful for the readers.

- I am also grateful to Swami Nirviseshananda and Ma Gurupriya for going through the script and for assisting in its finalization.

- I am grateful to my wife Aruna Mittal who has stood with me firmly all through my spiritual journey despite its very difficult terrain. But for her sacrifices, my enlightenment would not have been possible.

- I am grateful to my niece Sandhya Prakash and her husband Dr. Vipul Prakash, Professor at IIT Roorkee, who not only helped a lot in preparing the text but also rendered valuable guidance in its contents.

- I am grateful to my personal staff at Kabir Peace Mission, particularly Mr. Prabhat Bhargava, who worked hard in giving proper shape to the text on computer.

- I am grateful to Dr. Kirti Narain for going through the manuscript of this book several times and making valuable contribution in finalizing its draft.

- I am grateful to Mr. Sanjiv Sarin for doing excellent work in editing this book.

- I express my gratitude to Shri S. K. Ghai for publishing this book beautifully and in a short time. He is the one who made me an author by publishing whatever came from my pen by divine inspiration.

- Finally, I am grateful to the readers of this book who chose to read it despite many other options before them. This is the real reward of my efforts.

Rakesh K. Mittal

Amit Mittal
24th September 1973 – 8th May 2013

Rohit Mittal
16th April 1978 – 16th October 2013

Dedication

This book is dedicated to the memory of our departed sons, Shri Amit Mittal and Shri Rohit Mittal. They came into our life, played their role and left for heaven at their chosen time. But for them, perhaps this Spiritual Journey would have never been there. While living, they were our sons, after leaving they became our guides.

Rakesh K. Mittal
Aruna Mittal

Impressions

In Srimad Bhagvata Mahatmym it is stated

साधूनां दर्शनं लोके सर्वसिद्धिकरं परं
(Sadhunam darsanam loke sarvasiddhikaram param)

meaning, the very sight of an enlightened Mahatma brings all-fold, exemplary benefits.

A meeting with Pujya Swami Bhoomananda Tirthaji at the residence of Late Sri. Balasubramanian at Delhi in August,1991, marked a new phase in the spiritual journey of Sri Rakesh Mittal. This is what he has captured in his latest book *25 Years of Guru Sannidhi –The Story of My Spiritual Journey.*

Generally "Guru Sannidhi" implies wholesome, devotional presence in the vicinity of one's Guru. Being in the Indian Administrative Service, with innumerable responsibilities, this was not obviously possible for him. But mentally, in thought and awareness, Guru's benign presence was with him all these 25 years. This alone had helped him and his wife Smt. Aruna to face, sublimate and accept the tragic end of their only two sons afflicted with spastic paraplegia. Guru bhakthi is the only denomination on which seeker's welfare, progress and fulfilment depend.

I am also an ardent devotee of Swami Bhoomananda Tirthaji and ever since I met him in October 2002, there has been a wholesome change in my outlook and attitude while performing my duties.

I have read most of the books written by Sri Rakesh Mittal and their underlining values and philosophy had a great influence on me. His latest book, *25 Years of Guru Sannidhi –The Story of My Spiritual Journey* vividly and intimately brings out how he has progressed towards spiritual maturity.

Impressions

I am sure this book of Sri Mittal will be a beacon and inspiration to many who are struggling to find peace and quietude within themselves.

Dr. E. Sreedharan
Principal Advisor
Delhi Metro Rail Corporation

*****

I had the pleasure of reading the script of this book of Shri Mittal. While going through it, I had the feeling of living with him and seeing what's happening with his life. I could feel the pain of a father who himself has been a topper, but his child unable to clear exams or an officer as Principal Secretary,Medical, unable to find solution to his children's medical problems. But with all that he performed his official duties to the best, all because of his positive approach to life and with guidance of his Spiritual Master, who made him understand that God had chosen him for this challenge and he was able to give them the best possible. All this led to an inspiration to build SMRITI BHAVAN in memory of Amit and Rohit, to be remembered fondly always. This is a great contribution to society for betterment through Kabir Peace Mission. I hope we all are inspired by him to accept challenges of life in a positive way.

This is a book which will be of great help to all seekers.

Savita Agarwal
Sr. Architect, Lucknow

*****

25 Years of Guru Sannidhi, Shri Mittal's rendition of his spiritual journey, is a beautiful and soulful book and I have thoroughly enjoyed reading it. Spiritual belief comes out so succinctly in this manuscript. It is all heart and unswerving faith in the higher self. The letters exchanged between Swami Bhoomananda Tirtha and him are a revelation of the unique relationship between the *Guru* and *Shishya*. The kind of personal losses he suffered would break even the strongest of the strongest. I have seen people losing faith in the Almighty and the Sadguru when faced with even minor problems in life. However, his belief in the higher consciousness not only remained steadfast, it got reinforced and strengthened. What comes across in the book is the emotional connect between Arunaji, his wonderful spouse, and he, with Swamiji. Indeed, a must-read for all seekers of truth and the essence of the human incarnation.

For me, reading the book was a spiritual experience and it taught me a lot. His journey from a sceptic to a *sadhak* is worthy of contemplation and leaves the reader with food for thought.

Dr. Kirti Narain
Educationist

*****

Sri Rakesh Mittal has been leading an exemplary life. His new book, *The Story of My Spiritual Journey*, is an essential read for all those who want to give their life a meaning and a purpose. Sri Mittal was an outstanding officer of the IAS, who had a very successful and distinguished career and was known for his sensitive handling of issues and empathy with people. In this book, Sri Mittal starts his journey with a record of his academic achievements and goes on to his choice of career. But more important, he talks of his self discovery and spiritual awakening. He took inspiration from saints like Deoraha Baba and Swami Chinmayananda and other spiritually conscious human beings. Above all, this book as an account of his relationships, spiritual evolution and progress as a human being under the guidance, mentorship and direction of his Guru—Swami Bhoomananda Tirtha. An ideal Guru-disciple relationship is evident in his exchange of letters and interactions.

Blessed with a scientific and rational mind, Sri Mittal has shown that it is important to be a good human being. His organization, Kabir Peace Mission, has championed the cause of positive thinking and attitude in life.

Each one of us can lead a meaningful life if we listen to our inner self and get the blessing of a Guru. Sri Mittal got both and reading about his spiritual journey is itself a spiritual experience.

Alok Ranjan, IAS (R)
Former Chief Secretary
Uttar Pradesh

*****

Impressions

I am grateful and honoured that Sri Mittal shared the manuscript of this book with me. Like all his previous books, this makes an excellent and easy reading, a book which you can read at one go. And like all his other books, this also needs to be visited again and again to derive it's benefits. It's a classic, nothing less.

One always felt that one has known the Mittals rather closely, but needless to say one was humbled at one's ignorance. One knew that The Mittals were very different, humble, sincere, contemplative, public spirited with a kind of purity rare to find, inspirational and extremely well liked. But it was illuminating to share with them their path to inner growth. Since they are ordinary people like you and me, working and struggling with mundane life, events and nature, this journey becomes even more poignant and inspirational. You are not dealing with someone far away, not dealing with something esoteric and otherworldly, but are dealing with your own kind, with comparable lifestyles, except that you now know that they have also been following a path in parallel, cherished by many but followed by a few.

Our scriptures tell us that "Life" has been granted to us to discover our real self. Some religions and religious teachers tell us that Real Self is no different than the Divine and others agree that one can try to reach the levels of a Realised Soul. Some postulate that you just have to realise your true nature by shedding ignorance and others aver that you can achieve the same by following disciplined, regulated and in many cases codified tenets which are enshrined in what are normally referred to as Religions.

Ever since we have decided to lead a community life as opposed to being just gatherers and hunters, ever since we have decided to grow in numbers, the need for a code of social conduct was a natural consequence, and Religion and Gods and Prophets were only a step away. It also followed naturally that certain conduct and activities which help maintain peace, prosperity and happiness will be termed as Good or Virtuous and those that spread discord, misery and disruption will be termed as Vices or Bad. Obviously you will be advised to follow the path of Virtue with a constant reminder that it's the more difficult path and may not give you immediate benefits but assures a long term and lasting happiness. It's also said that the realisation may not happen in one life time but they assure you that this path is worth following since this path alone will make you rise beyond your mundane existence. Sri Mittal puts it beautifully when he says that the goal of human life is to achieve divinity and your body, mind, intellect and spirit, all need to be developed to achieve this ultimate goal. To that extent, following this path becomes an end in itself, with or without the promise of a Godhood or Heaven.

Sri Mittal also described this narrative as a Case study and I completely agree with him. It's rare to come across a person whose life has been a consistent and conscious effort for change towards the better in a spiritual sense. It's also not given to everyone to pass through such difficult tests as living with the constant fear of the loss of two wonderful loving sons. It's also not given to everyone to be in a position to have the best of times(his being in IAS) and sacrifice them all. It's also rare that one converts all calamities into a path of spiritual progress and social outreach. That one can grow beyond the limitations of me and myself, and create viable models of social good and spiritual progress is what this narrative amply proves. To that extent this becomes an exemplar.

One is also greatly benefited by the access to the correspondence between the Master and the worthy disciple. And since these happened decades ago under normal circumstances, one can appreciate the impact that pure and sincere guidance can have on one's life. It didn't take The Master much time to see that the Disciple is ready for initiation and instruction, and it must have also given him immense pleasure to see that his faith has not been misplaced.

One reads about the lives of Living Masters, but it's rarely that we come across the confessions of a true disciple, and this narrative is something which actually can lead many on to the right path. To that extent, the disciple, who has long since become a respected Mentor, has now become a Master. And this is what all Gurus want and secretly pray for. And the best part is that the Mittals have many more years to guide us.

Arun Kumar Misra, IAS (R)
Former Secretary to Government of India

*****

This book, written as a "Spiritual Biography" by Shri Mittal, takes us to the various facets of human life as it moves on, and goes up and down. In some cases the movement is faster and poses many questions about life. Their answer lies in spiritual wisdom only. Our mind has capacity to accept hardships and pains coming in its way and can maintain its poise. The *samsar* is dubbed as *maya* as it is ever changing and perishable.

This book provides ample answers to these questions as one goes through it. It has also strengthened my belief about the motherly care of a *Sadguru* in one's life. I feel enlightened, though still in the process of grasping the deep messages coming out from the book.

Dr. Krishna Behari Agarwal
President, Kabir Peace Mission

*****

ॐ नमो भगवते परमात्मने नमः।

Preface

This book is a story of my spiritual journey which practically began in 1980 and eventually brought me to the holy feet of my spiritual guide, Swami Bhoomananda Tirtha, in the year 1991. Since then, 25 years have passed and my life has been an ongoing journey on the spiritual path. During this period not much has changed in me externally, that is, my dress, my daily routine and even my beliefs, but internally, I have been increasingly at peace with myself and my environment. I can very modestly claim that equanimity now prevails in my life to a great extent and I feel that the credit goes to my spiritual master. Though the physical distance between our homes is enormous, we have met with each other on various occasions on his visits to various places, mainly Delhi (Vasundhara), Kanpur, Lucknow, etc. I have been to his Ashrama, called *Narayanashrama Tapovanam*, in Thrissur, Kerala, several times. Each association has given me more and more clarity about life and in a way reinforced it continuously. This has resulted in equanimity within me.

In February/March 2016, I visited Narayanashrama Tapovanam with my wife, Aruna, and spent few days in the *sannidhi* of our *Gurudev*. Suddenly it occurred to me that our association will be completing 25 years in November this year, as we were initiated on November 3, 1991, in Delhi. When I look back, it has been a very exciting journey; hence, I put the idea of writing a book on my spiritual journey on the auspicious occasion of our 25 years of association before *Gurudev*. Not only did he permit me to do so, but also blessed this effort.

Encouraged by this, I am venturing into writing of this book. The idea is to establish that each life has its own path, which ultimately takes it to the final destination of self realization. But out of our ego, we keep interpreting it in our own way and also interfere with it. This only results in delay in reaching the destination. What I realized was that *Sadguru* guides us to reach the goal early, provided we surrender in the true sense. Also, my *Sadguru* never demanded a blind surrender; he always gave a scientific and logical explanation to every doubt.

In my spiritual journey, many other saints and wise persons have played an important role and they will find mention in this book. But looking back, I am always amazed to observe how the events of life are interconnected and are an outcome of complex permutations and combinations. Yet, there is no such thing like chance or accident. I believe that each event of life is a logical process and is just. In our ignorance we start judging the events with our limited ego. When this judgment ceases, we start living a true life and feel blessed in all situations. This is what I learnt from all my guides in general and Swami Bhoomananda Ji in particular.

The association with Ma Gurupriya and Swami Nirviseshananda Tirtha has also played a great role in my spiritual journey. I came in their contact right during my first meeting with *Gurudev* in October 1991. At that time they had not taken *sanyasa deeksha* but were in the process of doing so. Their qualifications, manners and affection, all indicated symptoms of true spiritual conduct. The way both of them led the *Narayanashrama Tapovanam* to its glory under the divine guidance of *Gurudev* merits chronicling their journey. All these observations shaped my life in a silent manner and I am equally indebted to them in my spiritual journey.

Today the subject of spirituality has become very confusing. Most of the people are not able to distinguish between being religious and spiritual and consider it something alien from day to day worldly life. A truly spiritual person will never feel so. On the other hand, he sees them as being complementary to each other. The role of a true master is to make the devotee realize this, so that one is able to take care of inner as well as external resources. As a matter of fact, between the two, the inner resources are more important and ultimately take us to the goal of life.

The purpose of this book is to pass on my conviction about the spiritual path to the reader. While each one of us has our own destined path, coming across the right book or the right person at the right time is also a part of a person's destiny. If this book is able to play this part even partially, the effort will be well rewarded. Since this book is the outcome of *Gurudev's* blessings, it must definitely have a purpose.

I bow my head at the holy feet of Swamiji, Ma and Swami Nirviseshananda Ji for all their blessings in my life. Jai Guru!

October 25, 2016   **Rakesh K. Mittal**

'Upvan'   Mob: 9415015859
1/14 Vishwas Khand, Gomti Nagar,   rakesh_mittal_2000@yahoo.com
Lucknow-226010

Blessings

On 28 Feb 2016, Sri Rakesh Mittal had come to the Ashrama, with Aruna, his Shrimati. They were present in our evening satsang in Vijnana Bhavan. Somehow that day, we had asked the participants, including my ascetic disciples, to speak about their own spiritual life, its benefits, citing their experiences in the field. At last, I asked Rakesh: "Would you like to speak?" Though with some hesitation, he got up and walked forward to the mike.

During his short narration, Rakesh expressed that he was intending to write on his association with me and how it had impacted his life at home, in the office, as well as in the society. When he was returning to his seat after narrating some instances from his life after receiving spiritual initiation (deeksha) from me, I encouraged him to write. I think he took up the thread and was on this book very soon. Rakesh has the habit of writing books fast. He is used to writing regularly.

True spirituality and spiritual wisdom are identified with the Vedic Upanishads. The Upanishadic Saint thinkers invariably conversed with seekers who came to them with ascetic aspiration and resolve. Dispassion towards world was also a driving force for them to seek the feet of the ascetic Knowers living in the forest. Thus time and leisure available to the seeker and Knower alike were abundant. In the solitude of woods thus transpired the Upanishadic thoughts and dialogues. The entire subject of Brahmavidya, the spiritual message of the Upanishads, is exposed in these dialogues.

The culture and tradition apparently continued unchanged for millennia until at last the end of dwapara yuga and the beginning of kali yuga, about 5,000 odd years ago. It was then that the famous Kuru dynasty got divided, due to personal greed and flair for domination, leading to the unprecedented Mahabharata war between the Yudhishtira brothers and Duryodhana brothers. After 13-year long preparation, during which Arjuna had acquired special skills and aids for the impending war, both armies marched to Kurukshetra. And Arjuna suddenly asked Krishna to drive his chariot to the front, so as to enable him to examine the armies and decide on his strategy.

Krishna obeyed and stationed the chariot in front of Bheeshma and Drona, the commanders of Duryodhana army. Their sight unnerved Arjuna totally, and he began to tremble and cry profusely lamenting that he would not fight. Keeping his weapons down, he sat in the chariot, unable to stand.

In response to this was Krishna's warfield dialogue with Arjuna, lasting less than 3 hours. Krishna with his timely words enlightened Arjuna, expanding his vision and empowering his spirits. Arjuna too participated in the dialogue, raising relevant questions and seeking answers to them. Krishna obliged, inspiring the listener every time and enhancing his vision and resolve to fight.

The summary message of the entire dialogue was: "therefore, you fight". Till then people knew perhaps of only the spiritual wisdom leading to renunciation and absorption in the inner realms of stillness. Here they found a startling difference. The wisdom of the soul applied to the context of a huge war, in which 4.5 million army personnel had assembled, each with the resolve to fight, kill or get killed, finding it to be their goal of life.

I have always highlighted that Geeta is not an ascetic gospel. Instead, it speaks of interactional excellence, giving timely energy, drive and resolve to anyone. It inspires us to live our life and act every time with resoluteness and discernment, never shunning activity or its objective. Krishna's vision also has the unique merit of transforming every activity to a spiritual saadhana, in which it equals, nay even excels, the ascetic life of inner absorption or stillness.

Rakesh has had enough opportunity to imbibe the spirit of this exposition. It is natural that the narration of a public administrator, Krishna, to another administrator, Arjuna, has all the parallels for our public administrators. The objective in Kurukshetra then as well as in different fields now, is administrative alone, no matter whether it was monarchy then and democracy now. Public administration is a complex task and mission, and the puzzles, paradox, challenges and risks in decision-making are nonetheless the same. Thus Rakesh must have been enriched greatly by his spiritual association and exposure.

Let me mention one instance I happened to hear from Rakesh about his attitude and service orientation, which should also enthuse our public administrators. It was a winter in Uttar Pradesh. He was working in a district as a Dy. Commissioner. One day he was riding somewhere in his car. On the way he noticed an old man on the side of a road, with a stick in hand. Instantly he asked the driver to stop the car, open the dickey and take a blanket from it. The driver brought the blanket. Rakesh got down, went to the old man, and placed the blanket in his hands and smiled. The old man was touched to the quick. He did not know whether to smile or not.

Rakesh got back to the car and drove off. I wondered: "O, there is provision for such instances of personal kindness and help in a government official's life!" The instance speaks for itself.

If all our administrative officers were so personal, touching and sensitive to the public needs, what a heaven Mother India would be!

It is important to remember that the entire budget money of lakhs of crores of rupees are sanctioned as well as spent by District and State Administrative officers. If the IAS team grows in their bond of fondness to the Motherland and its subjects, every time interpreting and implementing the laws and provisions of the country to the actual benefit of people, and a people-friendly attitude is reflected by them, what would be the peace, orderliness and progress of the country! Our administrators can do an immense deal in building and ensuring the welfare of the Nation.

I had told Rakesh that his writing should help the readers to incorporate the interactional benefits and excellences which the study and pursuit of Geeta provide. I hope the writer has met this fundamental objective.

As for many other publications of Rakesh, for this too I am writing these words with a note of appreciation and blessings. May the readers have all inspiration and enlightenment to enrich their life and serve the society with greater heartiness and fondness, and the country advance steadily in all fields of National life.

Love and ashirvaad.
Swami Bhoomananda Tirtha

Narayanasrama Thapovanam,
Venginissery, P.O. Paralam,
Trichur, Kerala,
India-680575
21st August, 2016

Other books by the same author

21 Laws of Positive Living
Rakesh K Mittal
978 81 207 2446 4   ₹125

The Power of Positive Management
Rakesh K Mittal
978 81 207 3107 3   ₹150

Positive Mind Therapy
Rakesh K Mittal
978 81 207 2895 0   ₹150

Positive Mind Power
Rakesh K Mittal
978 81 207 2894 3   ₹150

Think Positive and Things Will Go Right
Rakesh K Mittal
978 81 207 2730 4   ₹90

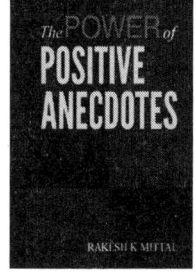

The Power of Positive Anecdotes
Rakesh K Mittal
978 81 207 7075 1   ₹200

Contents

	Gratitude	iii
	Impressions	vi
	Preface	xiii
	Blessings	xv
1.	Childhood and Early Career	1
2.	Spiritual Sprouting and Various Influences	6
3.	The Journey Continued	15
4.	Kabir Peace Mission	20
5.	A Worldly Storm and Guru Sannidhi	28
6.	Early Correspondence with Swamiji	34
7.	First Visit to Ashrama	66
8.	Swamiji Visits Kanpur	69
9.	Turning into an Author	78
10.	Disharmony at Home	81
11.	Transfer to Kolkata and First Guru Poornima Retreat	87
12.	Inspiration for Second Book	95
13.	More Developments at Home	99
14.	Establishment of CIRD in Delhi	102
15.	More Writings and Books	104
16.	Swamiji Visits Lucknow	117
17.	Administration as Sadhana	119
18.	Role of Spirituality in Administration	124
19.	Journey after Retirement	128
20.	Smriti Bhavan	141
21.	Inference	147
22.	About Swamiji and His Mission	151
23.	Some Enlightening Write-ups of Swamiji	158

Childhood and Early Career

Childhood

I was born in a family which was neither religious nor spiritual. My parents were almost illiterate, though my father could write some Hindi and Urdu. We were told that he studied up to class III, but my mother never went to school. My father was considered to be a pious person, who always thought well of others and always helped them to the best of his capacity. I never saw him going to a temple or carrying prayer beads or lighting a lamp before any deity. Yet he believed in God and never worried about the future. He was a very content person and felt rich in whatever came to him in the normal course. We always had a feeling of abundance in the family.

My mother, on the other hand, used to sit for *pooja* in the morning as well as in the evening, but only for short periods. Even during that period her attention used to be on household activities, and if there was anything urgent, she would give up her *pooja*. As mentioned earlier, she was unlettered, but she was a very affectionate and loving mother who could make any sacrifice for her children and family. Ours was a nuclear family and there was no influence of any elderly person within the family.

There were some persons in the town, close to our family, who were considered to be very religious. The main criteria of this qualification was their indulgence in temple visits, a string of prayer beads in their hands, frequent visits to Haridwar, which was close to our town, and fasting on various days. However, I noticed no reflection of this religiosity in their day-to-day conduct. I clearly remember the case of an old lady who we used to call *Bua* (father's sister). She was regularly among such religious persons, but when it came to her conduct, there were many noticeable aberrations. Despite several baths in a day, she was very dirty. She used to lie and quarrel with her daughters-in-law.

I was not even ten when I began observing these things and felt totally confused about the purpose of religion. For me, my father was the role model and I developed a faith in his value system without knowing whether it was religion or anything else. The habit of going to temples, keeping fast on various festivals (it was only optional and that too, a partial fast) or chanting of mantras was never inculcated in the siblings. As they grew older, they chose their own paths and lived accordingly. But none of us went astray. We lived a life well within the norms of an ethical society.

However, the impact of such an environment was more on me and I grew up almost as an atheist, never going to a temple, or keeping any fast or chanting any mantra. I just followed the value system I had observed in my parents.

I was good in studies and sports. As a result, my student life passed smoothly and successfully. I stood first in class in almost all my examinations, including the entrance exam of IIT Roorkee, which used to be conducted as a separate examination but under the umbrella of the University of Roorkee. I maintained my first position all through and emerged as the best student of the 1969–70 batch of the University. I was awarded several gold and silver medals, one of them for the best student at work and play. However, the pleasure of all these achievements was short lived.

At this stage there was no proper career guidance and I was not smart enough to explore the best possibilities for myself with regard to either a career or further studies. The means of doing so were also not available at that time, As a result, I landed a job in October 1970, which was not destined to be my career, and I started realizing that soon after joining.

Early Career

Being the youngest in the family, there was pressure on me to marry early and I willingly succumbed to it. My father was seventy-two at that time and wanted to free himself of his responsibilities. As a result, I got married on June 19, 1972, when I was not even twenty-three. My wife was an educated girl, coming from an established business family, but unaware of my frustrations. Very soon she came to know the uncertainty of my career, but vowed her full support in my ventures.

It was at this juncture that I started appearing for various competitive examinations. In August 1972 I appeared for the central government engineering examination and got selected for a Class I service, which I joined on May 1, 1974. Meanwhile, I had appeared for the Civil Services Examination in October 1973 after the birth of my elder son. I got selected, but for a service that did not satisfy me. I again appeared for the Civil Services Examination next year and, this time, got a good rank which enabled me to not only join the IAS, but also get my home cadre.

This was the end of my career search, the credit for which also goes to my wife Aruna, who was supportive all along and cooperated with me despite many difficulties. Finally, I could look forward to a life which gave me opportunities to serve the society. This wish of mine was not merely emotional but represented my long-held belief, as I mentioned in the TV interview taken after my selection.

I joined IAS training at Mussourie Academy on July 13, 1975, separated from my wife and son. They joined me occasionally for short durations whenever it was feasible and permissible. The training was for two years, out of which one year was in the field. During this time my family was always with me. In the final phase of my training in Mussourie, I was diagnosed with diabetes. I was not even 28 at that time and was least prepared to accept many life-long restrictions. It took me quite some time to come to terms with my diabetes. But, as will be revealed subsequently, I saw the grace of God in all these developments. Moreover, the excitement of entering the job that entailed public service overpowered all these issues and soon I was looking forward to my career.

It will be pertinent to mention one thing here. After marriage, while my wife used to visit temples to pray for me and also to follow various rituals at various festivals, etc., I had no such inclination even at that time. Usually, I would stand outside the temple and my wife would complete the rituals. Somehow, the impressions of my childhood still had an impact on my mind. At the same time, I had not felt the need to know about religion or spirituality. The only thing I knew was that a person should be good and do his work honestly, but without knowing why. Also, I felt no need to go deeper into this question.

In this background, I got my first posting as SDM (Sub Divisional Magistrate) in District Aligarh. In April 1978, I was posted as Additional District Magistrate (ADM) in Meerut, which was an important district adjacent to my home district, Muzaffarnagar. In June 1979, I was promoted at Meerut itself and posted as Secretary of Meerut Development Authority (MDA). This was a newly created office and was in bad shape. At both Aligarh and Meerut I served to the best of my capability, with full integrity. This had its impact and I got a lot of love and respect from people. There were some bitter experiences also, but these are part and parcel of an administrative career. Overall, I was quite happy with my performance and so were my bosses.

Childhood and Early Career

This post at MDA entailed direct interaction with people and had plenty of scope for corruption. Such thoughts never appeared in my mind, what to say of giving heed to them. On the other hand, I used to go the extra mile in helping the people. All this created a very good environment in the office as well as in the city. However, there were some people who suffered due to the transparent and honest working of the office, but they were in a miserable minority!

*****

2

Spiritual Sprouting and Various Influences

Spiritual Sprouting

In March 1980, I was transferred from Meerut to Lucknow. While shifting to Lucknow was personally inconvenient to me, I accepted the transfer and started preparing to leave. During this period a doctor friend of mine invited my family for a quiet dinner along with another friend of his who was an Income Tax lawyer. This friend appreciated my honesty and hard work, but expressed his doubts about the prudence of such an approach. In fact, his clear belief was that such persons repented later. Perhaps it was not his fault and it was the general feeling which prevailed in the society and seemed to be increasing with time. I gave no response to this observation but silently thought that it could be better to turn dishonest than repent for the honesty later. But this was not a solution to the problem and I wanted to go into the depth of the whole issue.

This was the moment when my spiritual sprouting took place. The first question which came to my mind was--What was goodness and why should one be good? Was there any logic in choosing goodness or was it a random choice? Related to these doubts were questions like--What is life and what

Spiritual Sprouting and Various Influences

is its purpose? Being a student of science I wanted scientific answers to all these questions. The traditional religion and its allied rituals could give no answers to me. But I became anxious to know the answers. With this state of mind, I moved to Lucknow and after a period of about four months moved to Gorakhpur in east UP as Regional Food Controller, which provided me ample time to contemplate.

Very soon we got comfortably settled in Gorakhpur. The house was spacious and comfortable. The post of Regional Food Controller, which I was holding, provided me opportunity to travel within the whole division, which was quite large. Occasionally, I could also travel to the state capital, Lucknow. Now I was looking forward to find answers to my questions. Fortunately, nature started assisting in this quest by bringing me in contact with the right persons, the right organizations and the right books. I shall briefly narrate the sequence of events.

Various Influences

My first interaction was with a General Manager of Railways who had just retired and was settled in my neighbourhood. He was associated with an organization called *Yug Nirman Yojna*, established by Shriramsharma Acharya, with headquarters at Shantikunj, Haridwar. The organization was spread all over the country as well as abroad. I found the philosophy of this organization quite scientific and its working transparent. Even their rituals were explained well and appeared logical. As a result of this, I also got associated with the organization and this association continues till today. I benefitted from reading quite a bit of literature written by Shriramsharma Acharya. In due course of time, I also met Acharya ji twice. Many of my doubts were removed as a result of these meetings. My family members also used to visit Shantikunj, Haridwar whenever it was possible and received lot of affection from Acharya ji and his wife, Mata Bhagwati Devi. I consider Acharya Ji to be my first spiritual master.

My second association at Gorakhpur was with Deoraha Baba whose Ashrama existed in Deoria district. This place was within my jurisdiction and it was easy for me to visit him frequently. I had known Baba because the family of a close friend of mine in Dehradun was his devotee. My first visit to Baba's ashrama was about two months after I joined my posting at Gorakhpur. It was the month of October, 1980. At that time some employees' problem was going on in my office and I was not in a very good state of mind. I wanted to share the problem with Baba and to seek his approval of my action plan. However, it took some time before Baba came out of his hut on to an elevated platform, but in the meanwhile, my mental agitation gradually receded. After listening to me Baba only said, "*Baccha sab theek hoga*" (my child, everything will be sorted out). It was a brief meeting as it was getting late in the evening and so Baba advised me to leave.

While returning to Gorakhpur, which was about a hundred kilometres from the Ashrama, my thoughts changed drastically. My anger towards my employees was now turning into compassion and I arrived at a conclusion that the problem was due to communication gap. When I reached home, it was already 9 p.m. and my wife was waiting for dinner. But before that, I wanted to talk to the employees' leader and called for him. He arrived soon and when I shared my heart with him, he was equally responsive. The problem was sorted out the very next day and our relations thereafter became very harmonious. As a result, official as well as personal life, both became smooth.

Thereafter I met Deoraha Baba many times, though our dialogues were never long. He hardly gave any formal sermon to his visitors and conveyed wisdom only through sporadic remarks. For some part of the year he used to be in Varanasi, Allahabad, Vrindavan and Rishikesh. In due course of time I had the opportunity to have his *darshan* at all these places. Baba had given me a *mantra* during our first meeting itself and it was considered to be the initiation process, though I had not taken it that way. However, I used to feel good in the company of Baba, and never put any worldly problems before him, nor did I expect anything from him.

Once in the summer of 1986, while Baba was camping at Allahabad during Kumbh Mela, I happened to visit him there. During this meeting, I had to wait for quite some time. Then Baba called me by name and after saying few words of appreciation for me, he suddenly said that I was capable of bearing any load happily without any complaint. I could not understand the implication of his words at that time, but perhaps he was signalling towards the difficult situations which we were going to face in our family in the form of my sons' disease. Our meetings continued after this also and perhaps the last meeting was in November 1989. By that time Baba had permanently shifted to Vrindavan following an ugly event at Deoria Ashrama.

Thus Deoraha Baba came to my life as another spiritual master and brought many subtle changes in my thinking. The ego of doing things came down drastically and with that came humility. This was all reflected in my office work also and I became a successful as well as a popular officer. I saw a direct connection between the two and that was an answer of my long sought question--Why should one be good? But there were some other persons also who played their role in this process.

The third person who influenced my life at Gorakhpur was Shri D. M. Sinha, a retired Civil Servant. Mr. Sinha had retired in February 1980 as Secretary, Food Department in UP government. During the course of his service, he had come in close contact with Shri Hanuman Prasad Poddar, who established Gita Press in Gorakhpur, and in that process had also come in contact with Radhe Baba who used to live in Geeta Vatika. Though Shri Hanuman Prasad Poddar had passed away by that time, Shri Sinha used to visit Radhe Baba from time to time. One of my officers was close to him and through him I also came in contact with Shri Sinha. Before that I had seen him when he had visited the Administrative Training Institute at Nainital while I was on training there.

Meeting Shri Sinha was a great experience at that stage of my life. He was a deeply spiritual person and, at the same time, a great administrator, musician, mathematician and, above all, a great human being. He removed many of my doubts in a very simple manner and my inclination towards spiritual quest increased a lot. This association also established the belief in me that good qualities of ours were our strength and they made our life better on all fronts.

My association with Shri Sinha deepened with time and continued throughout his life and beyond. With him I visited Geeta Vatika several times and came in contact with Radhe Baba. He also influenced me a lot with his spirituality and affection. Though he was quite an educated person, he was very simple in looks and humble in behaviour. I also noticed that many persons who occupied high positions in society were his devotees. This made me believe that spirituality in life was a higher state than our mundane status and only fortunate ones were chosen for this path.

Shri Sinha had a good command on Bhagavad Gita and explained it in a very simple manner. He made me curious to know more about Gita and this opened further doors for me as would be evident from the chain of events which followed. I also became an instrument in publishing Shri Sinha's own commentary on Gita under the title *Shrimad Bhagwad Gita Jeevan Vigyan*, both in Hindi and in English. This will be explained in greater detail later. For now, I am shifting to other influences on me during my stay at Gorakhpur.

In the month of November 1980, I accidentally came across a book titled *Kindle Life* by Swami Chinmayananda. It was kept in the room of a young IAS officer, Mr. Arun Kumar Mishra, from Orissa, who had come in my contact at Aligarh and had become a family friend. At that time he was also posted at Gorakhpur. While leaving for Orissa for getting married, he had requested me to get his suite in the officers' hostel properly arranged. I was getting it done under my personal supervision and while doing so came across this

Spiritual Sprouting and Various Influences

book in his room. It drew my attention immediately and I started glancing through it. This book was in the form of small lessons on life written in a very logical manner. For the first time, I had come across such an appealing book and I took it for reading. The book was so absorbing that I finished it within a few days. This book also removed my doubts to a great extent, but I wanted to know more about life. For this Swami Chinmayananda himself had advised the study of his book *The Holy Geeta* which was his detailed commentary. I started trying to find this book.

Providence provided me this book within a fortnight through another friend of mine, N. N. Upadhyaya, my IAS batch mate, who was also at Gorakhpur and lived in my neighbourhood. Towards the end of November 1980 he had gone for a training course to Goa and returned in the first week of December. He had purchased this book of Swami Chinmayananda there and when he returned from Goa with this book, I was waiting in the corridor of his residence. I almost jumped with joy when I saw this book in his hand and compelled him to lend it to me. He not only did that, but after a week or so presented it to me with love and regards. Perhaps my keenness for the book was appreciated by him and I have always felt grateful for this gesture of his. This book is a valued possession of mine till today. Later, on January 26, 1987, Swami Chinmayananda ji signed this book at Kanpur with a personal message, thus making it even more valuable for me.

As mentioned earlier, the nature of my job at Gorakhpur had provided me enough opportunity to read and reflect and I made the best use of it. It took me about a year (1981) to complete the study of *The Holy Geeta*, and it turned the course of my life. I could never imagine that this scripture of ours had such a powerful message for life. I had received a copy of the bare text of the Gita at the time of my admission to the University of Roorkee in 1966, but had never read it. Only after reading the commentary of Swami Chinmayananda, the importance of Gita was realized by me. It would also not be proper to say that one reading of the commentary made things clear to me, but it opened the door for more and more spiritual wisdom. Subsequently, reading a few pages of this book every day became a part of my daily routine and this habit continued for decades.

Another development which took place during my initial period at Gorakhpur was a visit to Maghar. This place fell in the neighbouring district of Basti but was only about 25 kilometres from Gorakhpur. This is the place where Kabir died and his mortal body is said to have transformed into flowers, which were shared by his Hindu and Muslim followers equally. Both communities followed their own rituals and today a *mazaar* and *samadhi* exist together there as a mark of Hindu Muslim unity.

In my first visit itself, I was deeply influenced by Kabir's personality. Though, I had some knowledge of him through school textbooks, I now wanted to know more about him and acquired some books on his life. I became a regular visitor to this place and always drew great inspiration from the life of Kabir. In years to follow, I became District Magistrate of Basti and in that capacity played an important role in the development of Maghar.

While the reading of the Gita commentary went on all through 1981, my interaction with Yug Nirman Yojana, Shri D. M. Sinha, Geeta Vatika, Maghar and Deoraha Baba also continued. All this reduced my interaction with my family and my wife was not very happy with this development. The general feeling that domestic life had a conflict with spiritual life prevailed in her also and I did not pay enough attention to this aspect. As a result, there were occasional conflicts at home which had an adverse effect on my family life. However, in this matter Shri D. M. Sinha was a great help. Whenever he came to Gorakhpur, he used to visit us and explain how spiritual and domestic life could enrich each other. Suffice will be to say that this conflict never crossed limits and my wife gave me full cooperation in my spiritual pursuit. In retrospect, I only feel that I should have taken her more into

Spiritual Sprouting and Various Influences

confidence as I did later. Perhaps, I myself was ignorant of many things in that early part of my spiritual journey.

At the end of 1981, I went to Mumbai and Goa with my wife and both sons. We spent the New Year eve in Goa and stayed with a friend there. My friend's family was very pious and I noticed very inspiring literature at their home. There I also came across a copy of *Bhavan's Journal*, a fortnightly magazine of Bharatiya Vidya Bhavan. I liked the contents of the journal and this brought me in contact with Bharatiya Vidya Bhavan. On the advice of my friend, I became its life member and started receiving its journal. I used to read each copy from beginning to end and gained a lot of wisdom from them. In due course of time I came in close contact with the secretary-general of Bhavan, Mr. S. Ramakrishnan, and met him several times in Delhi as well as in Mumbai. He grew fond of me and our closeness continued till his death. In later years, Bharatiya Vidya Bhavan published English commentary on Gita by Shri D. M. Sinha, as mentioned earlier. I was also involved in creating the Lucknow centre of Bhavan and in reviving its Kanpur centre.

In short, my association with Bharatiya Vidya Bhavan also played an important role in my spiritual journey. Through its articles I learnt about various saints and socio-religious organizations of the country. It made me realize that India had deep-rooted religious and spiritual traditions. It was only towards the latter half of the 20th century that material considerations had started overshadowing them. Since religion and spirituality was not being explained or projected in a proper manner, the beliefs expressed by my friend at Meerut, that good persons generally repent their being good, were gaining roots. Thus, things were not only becoming clear to me, I also started feeling the need of working in this field.

Bharatiya Vidya Bhavan has published a large number of good books. I became fond of them and acquired many of them. My initial reading started with *Ramayana* and *Mahabharata* written by Shri C. Rajagopalachari, the first

Governor General of India. Till then I had only read *Ramayana* in a traditional manner without going into its depth and had only heard some short stories from *Mahabharata*. After reading these two books of Rajaji, for the first time I had the feel of the depth of our traditional scriptures and realized their relevance towards creation of a good and ethical society.

I found both these books very relevant for my administrative career also. Not only this, my reverence towards my country increased a lot because I realized that a large number of our countrymen followed these scriptures in their lives. Even religious rituals now did not repel me as much as they used to earlier. After reading these books I only felt that traditional practices needed amendments from time to time and that was possible only through spirituality. In any case, my conflict had come down to a great extent.

*****

3

The Journey Continued

From Gorakhpur, I was transferred to the neighbouring district of Basti as District Magistrate. This was my first appointment on this post and like every IAS officer I also looked forward to work with great zeal. Basti was the biggest district of the State at that time and also one of the most backward districts, socially as well as economically. I served this district to the best of my capability as well as full integrity and that was my main *sadhana*. I remained on the post for about two years and got full satisfaction from my work. Like every human being, I also made some mistakes, but those were without any ulterior motive and so caused no harm to me. On the other hand, I earned tremendous goodwill and love of the people and I cherish this till today. These developments also increased my conviction in goodness.

My next posting was as the Joint Development Commissioner of Garhwal, for which I had given my consent. While doing so, I did not know the difficult conditions of Garhwal and my only consideration was that the Himalayas would provide me a better environment for my spiritual development. I was wrong in that respect. The personal difficulties faced by me during this posting were far more than the congenial environment of Himalayas. My family was not comfortably settled and frequent travel in hilly terrain was not a pleasure at all. Of course, I got an opportunity of visiting many religious places like Rishikesh, Devprayag, Rudraprayag, Karnprayag, Badrinath, Kedarnath, Gangotri, Yamunotri, and so on. But I realized that in the absence of a peaceful mind, they hardly provided any spiritual progress.

During this time I came in touch with Divine Life Society and met Swami Krishnananda, the head of the organization at that time. He gave me several books and I read most of them, getting benefited in the process. This period made me realize that one should leave the journey of life to the process of nature and accept what comes in its way. After this I never applied my mind to seeking a particular post in my career and I never regretted that.

I was transferred to Kanpur in June 1985, as Additional Director of Industries. At that time it was an important job and I had good public interaction. Gradually, I started making many friends due to my reputation as an honest and hardworking officer. Still, my spiritual journey was on and I was continuously looking for the right individuals, the right books and the right organizations. The job at Kanpur provided me with ample opportunities to do so.

From Kanpur I used to travel to Lucknow frequently for attending official meetings. There I came in contact with Ramkrishna Mission and its literature. The life of Swami Vivekananda influenced me a lot and I acquired many books of this mission including *Complete Works of Swami Vivekananda*. I read biographies of Swami Ramkrishna Paramhansa, Ma Sharda and Swami Vivekananda. These books gave me a great insight into the possibilities of a spiritual life. The reading of *Complete Works of Swami Vivekananda* continued for a long time. All this resulted in my closeness to Ramkrishna Math, which continues till now. What I liked in particular was that spirituality and social service should go together.

During the same period I also came in contact with *Gandhi Sansthan* at Lucknow. We all know Gandhi as the Father of the Nation and a great man, but what made him so great is generally not understood. I had the desire to know more about Gandhi and the first book which helped in this respect was his autobiography, *My Experiments with Truth*.

I believe that the same book can give you different insights depending upon the keenness and purpose of the reader. When I read this book at that stage, it was almost a revelation. Gandhi was an ordinary person to begin with, but he became extraordinary by strictly following certain principles in his life--truth and non-violence were the most important amongst them. The inference of the book was that when one honestly follows the path of truth, even our weaknesses turn into strengths, provided we work for a selfless purpose. Thereafter I read a lot of literature on Gandhi, including his book, *Satyagraha in South Africa*. This book further strengthened my belief that if we work selflessly and transparently for a genuine cause, we get cooperation from all quarters. However, it is easier said than done, but that is what turned Mohandas Karamchand Gandhi into Mahatma Gandhi.

Thus, these personalities, namely, Kabir, Vivekananda and Gandhi, influenced me the most and I always thought of acquiring as many of their qualities as possible. I knew that it was to be a lifelong process, but that is what the purpose of life is.

I also read a large number of biographies and autobiographies in due course of time and learnt lessons from all of them. Some prominent ones are— Aristotle, Shri Aurobindo, Jamnalal Bajaj, Annie Besant, Vinoba Bhave, Justice P. N. Bhagwati, Subhash Chandra Bose, Gautam Buddha, Albert Einstein, Indira Gandhi, Dalai Lama, Abraham Lincoln, Ramana Maharshi, Nelson Mandela, Dr. K. M. Munshi, Jawaharlal Nehru, Prabhu Pad, Nani Palkhiwala, Sardar Patel, C. Rajagopalachari, Shri Rajneesh, Rabindranath Tagore, J. R. D. Tata, Mother Teresa, Lokmanya Tilak, George Washington, and many others. All these personalities enriched my life in one way or the other.

My six year stay at Kanpur also provided me a good opportunity to travel extensively in India and abroad. During the course of these travels I met many people, which gave expansion to my inner personality. I would like to mention a few of these people. One was Baba Amte, whose leprosy centre, *Anand Van*, I visited in May 1988. Though I could not meet him personally, for me it was unbelievable that compassion could reach to that level. I was also very influenced by Dada J. P. Vaswani of Sadhu Vaswani Mission at Pune. His humility touched me to the core. I also had the chance of visiting Anna Hazare in his native village. At that time he was in the process of developing his village and had succeeded to a great extent. Another personality who influenced me was Medha Patkar. Apart from these, there were many lesser known personalities who were doing selfless service in the society in various fields. These people inspired me a lot to serve the society, rising above narrow considerations.

This was the time when Shri D. M. Sinha recorded about 20 audio cassettes of ninety minutes containing a commentary on Gita. It was in very simple language, mainly meant for householders. I had also acquired a set of these cassettes and often played them during my journeys between Kanpur and Lucknow. In this way, in the span of about four years, I had listened to the whole commentary several times and got benefited immensely.

One day the idea of converting these cassettes into the form of a book came to my mind. To begin with, I tried to do it at my level but failed to do so. Then I approached Shri Sinha personally and implored him to undertake the task of converting these recorded cassettes into the form of a book. After initial hesitation, he accepted my request and within a few months converted the oral commentary in the form of a beautiful book, titled, *Shrimad Bhagwad Gita - Jeevan Vigyan*. This book was published by Kabir Peace Mission about which I am going to write shortly. This was another important stage in the direction of my spiritual journey.

While I was cherishing my spiritual pursuits, some incidents took place in my official life which made me think about my identity. In July 1987, I was posted to an important post in Kanpur and was doing very well when there was a sudden transfer because of political reasons, but I was given another good post in Kanpur itself. The same thing happened again after a year and I was transferred to another post in Kanpur for the same reasons. These developments made me think about my real identity. Most of us think of our identities on the basis of external acquisitions but if they are so transitory, how can one have an identity based on them? This development, perhaps, was to raise me further from the temptations of external positions—a growth so essential for a rapid spiritual journey.

*****

4

Kabir Peace Mission

Meanwhile, my concepts about human life were getting clearer and most of my questions had been answered by one source or the other. I could now speak about the strength of goodness with much more conviction and wanted to respond to the comment of my friend at Meerut who advised me to rethink about my good qualities. I, therefore, first collected my thoughts in the form of an article, titled, "Why to be Good?" I widely circulated this write up and a got very positive response. I am producing this paper here also.

Why to Be Good

Today, the life of man has become so complicated that he has lost sight of its primary goal. In this confusion, he has started believing that there is no point being good and that good people are generally unsuccessful and unhappy. I got the inspiration to think over this matter quite some time back. At that time I was posted in a sensitive post. On my transfer from there, during a farewell dinner at a friend's place, a common friend of ours showed his concern by saying that I had worked very hard and honestly on that job but such persons generally regretted in the end. I was taken aback by his remark and did not know what to say. Perhaps I was not in a position to say anything. Otherwise also, I had never thought on this subject. What he said was perhaps the common viewpoint and he could not be blamed for that. At that time I only said that it was better to be dishonest than to regret being honest.

However, I was not satisfied and started thinking as to why one should be good. Was there any science of goodness? I have been a student of science and do not accept anything illogical. Hence I needed proper explanation of the same. During this search I came across some spiritual books which have been written very scientifically. In fact, I got the correct definition of "religion" from these books as well as the answer to my query. Not that every doubt got removed immediately, but the fundamentals became clear. The doubts which arose in course of time were also removed as a result of study and experience. Today, I can say with full conviction that it is fortunate to be a good person and in all situations goodness is strength and not weakness. However, it needs discussion as to how one should face today's society so that his goodness brings him respect instead of making him a laughing stock.

First of all, one should know the meaning of "goodness". Generally the mistake is committed here itself. In all parts of the world, one religion or the other is followed. After all, why did we need religion? As mankind developed and formed society, the need for a set of rules of life was felt. Religion was the result of this need. In a way, mankind got religion in the form of "Constitution of Life". With the change in the circumstances, amendments were required in this constitution and, as a result, new religions came into being. However, there are certain cardinal principles which are same in all religions. We may call them fundamental principles of life. There can hardly be any difference of opinion on these principles. In my view, to follow these fundamental principles of life is "goodness". This way goodness is a social need more than an individual need. It is necessary not only for individual happiness but for social happiness too. Unfortunately, this faith is getting eroded while no alternative is suggested for social as well as individual happiness. As a result, man today is in such a dilemma where he does not know how to achieve happiness. By the time he realises that happiness lies in following the path of goodness only, generally it is too late.

To establish a relationship between "goodness" and "happiness" it would be necessary to contemplate upon certain points. Though one may take a very philosophical view on the subject, we shall confine ourselves to its practical aspect only in this discussion. The first question which comes to everyone's mind is "what is the goal of human life?" The most realistic answer to this would be that "attainment of happiness" is the goal of human life. The next question arises, "what is happiness?" There can be several answers to this question and it will depend upon the intellectual development and experience of an individual. Therefore, it needs some explanation so that some sort of consensus may be brought on the definition of happiness. I would only like to say there is no definite relationship between material prosperity and happiness. It cannot be said with certainty that a materially prosperous man is always happy or vice versa. For example, wealth may be a cause of happiness but it can equally be a cause of misery. A son may be a cause of happiness but he can equally be a cause of misery. A high position may be a cause of happiness but it can equally because of misery. We can give several such examples. These examples are not merely for the sake of argument but these are the facts of life which no one can deny. Thus there should not be any doubt that happiness is a state of mind and the goal of human life is to achieve that state of mind.

Now the question is how to achieve such state of mind and if there is any way, following which one can achieve such state of mind, it is advisable to follow that path only. If we take these criteria as a touchstone, the dilemma of life will disappear. However, it is necessary to be honest while judging ourselves on this touchstone and there should be no cleverness. If we do so, we shall deceive none but ourselves. It can be said with certainty that anything which does not fall in the category of goodness will fail on this touchstone. If we want to achieve the mental state of happiness, there is no option but to follow goodness. This way, by being good, we favour none but ourselves. For example, if we do not carry a feeling of revenge, we get more benefited than anyone else. Similarly, if we follow truth, we are the first beneficiary. Several such examples can be given. On the other hand the path of evil can never lead to that state of mind which we are seeking. This can also be confirmed by several examples.

From the above, it appears that if happiness is achieved so easily by following the path of goodness, why does everyone not follow the same? Essentially, the nature of man is this only but it is not easy to discriminate between the path of goodness and the path of evil. Everyone feels that what he is doing will lead to happiness. Only a fortunate few are able to look and think beyond their immediate surroundings. Generally, the path of evil is more attractive in the beginning than the path of goodness. Due to this attraction one starts following the same. He also finds this path to be more crowded which removes his doubt. Once on the path of evil, he tends to remain there either due to ignorance or, perhaps, it is too late to change the course. While he knows his mistake, he does not admit it. Not only this, he discourages others too from following the path of goodness by giving them a false image of his happiness. As a result those who want to follow the righteous path either do not follow it at all or leave the same midstream. Then they also start advocating against the path of goodness. The suggestion given by my friend in the beginning is applicable to such persons who give up the path of goodness in the mid-course. Those who complete their journey on this path cannot even think of regretting it.

In the end, it is necessary to contemplate upon how to face today's world while being on the righteous path. I will mention here a line from the book *The Inner Reality* by Paul Brunton. While discussing the similar situation he has said, "Be ye harmless like a dove, but wise as serpent". This clarifies the whole approach. While it is necessary not to harm others, it is also necessary not to get harmed as a result of our goodness. However, it should be clearly understood whether the situation which we take as harmful is in reality so or not and whether it adversely affects us and the society. If yes, we should oppose it with firmness and establish that the righteous path is our strength and not weakness. This kind of firmness is very essential in today's world. It should also be kept in mind that a person on the path of evil is a weak person and normally our firmness is enough to beat him. But if our goodness gives an impression of weakness, the fault lies with us and we have to remove this fault by proper introspection.

Thus it is proved that in order to achieve the goal of life, there is no alternative but to follow the righteous path. In the short run, the goal may not be visible, but it is finally achieved on this path only. This is an eternal truth like any scientific principle.

This paper was circulated widely and the process goes on even now. Though all seem to agree with the logic given, most feel that practising goodness in life is becoming difficult with time. In such a situation, understanding spirituality becomes necessary, which only removes our dilemma and provides reinforcement to our personality. This was the main objective before me.

It was in September 1989 when I was transferred for the second time within Kanpur, as mentioned earlier. By this time I had completed more than four years there and had made many good friends. They all appreciated my sincerity and urge to do something for the society. My wish was to share my conviction with others and to remove ignorance prevailing about goodness in life. For this I wanted to create an organization which would have no conflict with my government job. I therefore drafted a paper on the issue and shared it with like-minded friends. It was appreciated in general and after ample discussion we arrived at a final draft. The four main friends who joined me in this initiative were Dr. Krishna Bihari Agrawal, Shri Bharat Bhushan Gupta,

Dr. Rajesh Agarwal and Shri Pradeep Goenka. We decided to create a trust in the name of "Kabir Peace Mission" with a one line motto, *A mission to develop positive thinking in the society.* We felt that instead of spiritual, positive would be a better word because spiritual was considered to be otherworldly, and we wanted to address this misconception also.

The mission was named after Kabir because he was above any religion, caste and creed. Man was the focus of our effort, and who could represent humanity better than Kabir? Moreover, he was one of the personalities who had influenced me the most and was acceptable to all. For us, peace was synonymous with holistic development because in the absence of peace, development had no meaning. This was possible only when the process of development is carried out with values and with everyone's welfare in mind. Mission, of course, implied that life had to be lived like a mission and every task should be undertaken with a missionary zeal. Thereafter, a trust deed was drafted and we formally adopted in on January 14, 1990, followed by its registration at Kanpur on February 8, 1990.

The next step was to launch the mission in a proper manner. Before doing so, we shared the philosophy of the mission with a large number of intellectuals in various fields and places. While soliciting their views we also approached them to become its members. Our target was to enrol about a hundred members before the formal launch.

The response was larger than our expectations. We decided to launch the mission on April 22, 1990, at Kanpur and to invite the then Governor of U. P., Hon'ble Shri Satyanarayan Reddy, as the Chief Guest. It was also decided to publish a quarterly journal of the mission under the title, *Kabir Jyoti*. The first issue was to be released during the launching ceremony. We also decided to release Shri D. M. Sinha's book, *Srimad Bhagavad Gita - Jeevan Vigyan*, on this occasion. Therefore, work was to be expedited at that front also.

Every one of us was working hard for the event. It was a big task for us, particularly when we were working on a new mission. In fact, many of our friends had serious doubts about its success, in the absence of any concrete agenda.

A new development took place in the first week of March 1990. My wife's younger brother's wife committed suicide in Delhi leaving all of us shocked and surprised. She was around 35 and never appeared depressed in her life. When we were returning from Delhi to Kanpur after this incident, we started thinking about the possible reasons for this extreme action. Our conclusion was that she must have been negative in her thinking. This is when I decided that we should be spreading positive literature in the society.

Immediately, I started collecting positive thoughts which eventually became more than a thousand in number. It was then decided to publish these in the form of a book under the title, *Dictionary of Positive Thoughts*, as they were placed alphabetically. It was also decided that this book should also be released on the day of launching of the mission. I remember working up to late hours for several nights in order to complete this book on time. Anyhow, the book was ready before the launching day, though not in a very attractive form. This was the mission's first publication and became very popular in due course.

The launching of the mission was very successful and the Merchant Chamber Hall was packed to capacity. Almost all dignitaries of the city attended the programme and it encouraged us immensely. Incidentally, I was to leave for a 12-week course in UK on April 24 and, therefore, we could not plan much for future course of action.

In my absence, some members informed about some confusion in the working of the mission. For me it was a godly mission and I was sure that an appropriate method of working would be carved out by nature itself. I responded to the members accordingly and they all decided to wait for my return. Meanwhile, work on the next issue of Kabir Jyoti was on.

I returned from the UK in the last week of July, 1990. The 12-week stay in the UK was very informative and useful, but I missed my family. My wife was not very comfortable being alone in Kanpur, but there was no way out. I tried to fill the gap by writing a letter every alternate day. In those days there was no facility of mobile phones and even ISD was not easily available. Of course, the joy of receiving a phone call or a letter in those days has no parallel in modern times of instant and frequent communication.

While I was in the UK, Deoraha Baba and Acharya Shriramsharma of Shantikunj passed away. I was shocked to hear this news. These were the two saints whom I had taken as my spiritual guides and with their departure, I felt spiritually orphaned. However, I did not think much about it and left the future of my spiritual journey on providence.

After returning to India I visited both the places to pay my homage to the departed souls. The work at Shantikunj had started going well under the guidance of Mata Bhagwati Devi and Dr. Pranav Pandya. I kept very close contact with both of them and their blessings were always with me and my family. Mataji, in particular, used to take very affectionate care of us. Deoraha Baba, of course, left no legacy in the form of a successor, but a group of his disciples continued to work to keep his teachings alive.

*****

5

A Worldly Storm and Guru Sannidhi

A Worldly Storm

In December 1990, I got transferred to another post in Kanpur itself. I had handled that post earlier also and so life became easier at the professional front. My elder son, Amit, was to appear for class 12 examination in March 1991 and so needed my personal attention. While I was trying to do so, a serious accident took place in which my sister's daughter and son-in-law were involved. The son-in-law died on the spot while the daughter got seriously injured. They both were at Kanpur, hence there was a lot of disturbance in the studies of Amit. Once again, we had to leave his future in the hands of nature.

My younger son, Rohit, was also not doing well in his studies and that was another worry for us. We failed to understand what was there in store for us and were only trying to seek the blessings of God amid all these worldly worries.

Simultaneously, another problem was developing with Amit, the gravity of which we were unaware of. He had started facing some difficulty in walking about three years back in mid-1987. Medically, it was suspected to be an orthopaedic problem and the doctors felt that it was due to his flat foot. Accordingly, measures were taken but there was hardly any improvement. On the other hand, his problem was getting worse. After his class 12 examination, we paid more attention to this problem and in April 1990 a neuro-physician of Lucknow was consulted, who declared it to be a case of neurology. After further investigation, she diagnosed it to be a serious problem, which, in medical terms, is known as "Spastic Paraplegia". The doctor also advised further examination at All India Institute of Medical Sciences (AIIMS) in Delhi. She said that it was a genetic disease and there was a fair chance of my younger son also developing the same.

This was like a storm in our life. Notwithstanding the spiritual clarity gained so far, these developments shook us and we did not know how to go about things in life further.

We made arrangements to go to Delhi for examination at AIIMS. On the day we were to leave for Delhi, I received the news about my appointment in the Government of India (GOI) in New Delhi. Normally, an officer's consent is taken before sending him to GOI, but in my case it was not done. My first response to this was of refusal, but in view of my sons' disease, I started having second thoughts. There was some advantage in continuing at Kanpur and some in shifting to Delhi. In addition to this, it was also a matter of my career, for which going to Delhi was a better option.

Amid this state of mind, my sons were admitted in AIIMS, New Delhi. After carrying out some tests, the disease was confirmed. The doctors also told us that the same would happen to our younger son as well. While in Delhi, I started exploring other arrangements like admission, accommodation, transport, etc., in case we were to shift to Delhi. Fortunately, all these arrangements were made without much difficulty and in view of the outcome at AIIMS, I decided to join at Delhi.

Amit had passed his class 12 and was to appear for some competitive examinations. Though the diagnosis of his disease had changed the course of his life, acceptance of reality came slowly. It was decided to leave him with a friend in Meerut, whose son was also to appear in the same competitive exams. My younger son got admission in Bharatiya Vidya Bhavan, New Delhi. We got a reasonably good accommodation in a guest house and a second hand car was purchased. With all these logistics taken care of, we moved to Delhi in the middle of July, 1991.

Guru Sannidhi

Slowly, we were coming to terms with the new situation. The guest house was comfortable and my wife had set up a small kitchen also. Regular accommodation was applied for and awaited. The guest house was located in the posh area of Hauz Khas very near IIT Delhi. I started going there for my morning walk. Amit had shifted to Meerut and Rohit started going to school in Delhi. Simultaneously, we were trying to explore all possible treatments for Amit. This was the time when I badly missed a living spiritual guide.

It was during this period that I met a retired Army Brigadier during my morning walks in the IIT Campus. We were impressed with each other. Very soon he could sense my spiritual inclination and suggested that I must meet Mr. Balan Subramanian, who was my neighbour in Hauz Khas. As providence was planning the same, the next day it was Mr. Subramanian who met me during the morning walk. He was an elderly person with a very serene look. Conversation with him was a delight and we kept on doing so for many days. I could not disagree with anything he said about life and its goal. All this was already ingrained in my thinking and so we grew close to each other very soon.

One Sunday afternoon, probably in the latter half of August, 1991, Balanji invited me and my wife for a cup of tea at his residence, which was only a few blocks away from the guest house. There we saw a photograph of a saint kept in a prominent place in the drawing room. It attracted both of

A Worldly Storm and Guru Sannidhi

us equally. Balanji told us that it was the photograph of his spiritual master, Swami Bhoomananda Tirtha, who lived in Thrissur, Kerala. He also told us that Swamiji visited Delhi every year in the month of October-November and stayed with them. He extended his invitation to attend Swamiji's programme when he came in October. Whatever description of Swamiji was given to us by Balanji and his wife touched our hearts, but we were not sure how things would turn out to be in the coming months. We were waiting for a regular government accommodation which could materialize any day.

In the first week of September, 1991, I went to a training programme at Administrative Staff College of India (ASCI), Hyderabad, for a week. During this period I bought a book of Shri Satyanarayan Goenka titled, *Art of Living*. In this book there was a chapter with the heading "Need of a living Guru". After reading this, I once again started missing a living spiritual guide. My only confusion was that having mentally accepted Deoraha Baba and Shriram Sharma Acharya as my spiritual guides, would it be appropriate to accept another living master? This confusion of mine was removed by Shri D. M. Sinha. He told me that all saints were the conduits of divine knowledge and transpired the same nectar as different taps do in a household water supply. With this clarification, I was now looking forward to having a spiritual guide, I was allotted a regular house soon after that. It was a decent accommodation in Asian Games Village. The allotment had come after a lot of persuasion and running around and refusal would have meant being out of the queue for an uncertain period. My wife was not very happy with this accommodation as it had split levels. She thought it would cause problem to our sons as well as to our parents, who were then alive and often lived with us. But she did not understand the implications fully and only reluctantly agreed to move there. We went to Kanpur to pick up our household luggage where it was lying packed. At this point she again expressed her doubts about the advisability of shifting to the allotted accommodation and in the process we started arguing. In view of this disharmony, I decided not to shift, whatever be the consequences and we returned to the Delhi guest house, leaving things in the hands of providence. Thereafter I made no efforts in the direction of house allotment.

With this came the month of October and Swami Bhoomananda arrived in Delhi and was hosted by Shri Balanji. In retrospect, I see a great hand of providence in all these developments. Swamiji used to give a discourse in the morning from 7 to 8 a.m. at Balanji's place, to which I was also invited. I was already looking forward to this opportunity and managed my morning routine in such a manner that after the morning walk, I reached for the discourse. As was anticipated, Swamiji's aura, his words and expression made an immediate impact on me. Every word of his enriched me profoundly and I was in perfect tune with him. After the talk, Balanji introduced me to Swamiji while receiving *prasadam*. Swamiji gave me a very affectionate look and asked me to come again. I had already planned to come daily and after three days my wife also came with me. She was equally influenced with Swamiji and his words. After the discourse, we prayed to Swamiji for a personal meeting to which he readily agreed, and fixed it for the afternoon of October 25, 1991.

Since it was a working day, I took a half-day leave from my office and reached for the meeting at the appointed time. By this time Swamiji had come to know of our sons' problem and my administrative background. He was accompanied by his two disciples, then known as Aroop Ji and Deepa Ji (now as Swami Nirviseshananda and Ma Gurupriya). At that time they had not taken the full *sanyasa* but were in that process. Even their disposition was very affectionate and soothing. We told them more about us and how we had started moving on the spiritual path for the past few years. I also gave details of my administrative and personal life. Swamiji listened to us very attentively and seemed pleased. Encouraged by this, words spontaneously came from my mouth expressing my wish to be initiated by him. Swamiji thought for a minute and proposed that it would be better to get to know each other more before the initiation process was carried out. As I was going to agree with this proposition, something transpired between Swamiji and Aroop ji, after which Swamiji gave his consent for our initiation. At that time we did not know much about the initiation ceremony, but only had faith that we were in safe hands. Immediately, the afternoon of November 3 was fixed for our initiation. After this Swamiji also met our sons and blessed them very affectionately. It was clear that Swamiji had no immediate answer to their problem. Perhaps he looked much beyond what we were not able to understand at that point of time.

As decided, my wife, Aruna, and I were initiated on November 3, 1991, which was a Sunday. It was a simple ceremony in which Swamiji gave both of us a *Diksha Mantra*. It was to be chanted mentally, as much as was feasible, and no strict regime was prescribed for the same. According to Swamiji, *sadhana* was required more at mental and intellectual levels than at the body level. This was what we also believed in and so there was a perfect understanding between us. Swamiji left for Thrissur after a few days and we felt a great void inside us. However, this association was to go a long way.

*****

6

Early Correspondence with Swamiji

At this point of time, I realized that it was not enough only to have spiritual clarity but what mattered more was how one lived that clarity. As far as concepts were concerned, they were, by and large, clear to me by the time I came in *sannidhi* of Swamiji. What was required was their absorption into my personality. It was like a building which appeared beautiful and strong in the absence of any calamity but if it had to stand tremors, floods, fire, etc., the design had to be altogether different. Similarly, it was easier to live gracefully when things went well in life. The test came when there were upheavals in life and ones' spiritual concepts were put to test. For my wife and me, it was this type of a situation and that is why providence brought us under the shelter of Swamiji. Fortunately the reinforcement process did not take very long and we could face events of life with equanimity soon. In this process, correspondence, personal interaction and discourses of Swamiji, all were very helpful. I wrote my first letter to Swamiji on November 17, 1991, from the guest house itself. I am sharing this letter in original.

K-114 Hauz Khas,
New Delhi – 110016
17.11.1991

Our most revered Swami ji,
Pranams,

    Our family is very fortunate to have come under your shadow during your stay in Delhi. We really wonder at the divine design of events when we think of it. My posting at Delhi, staying in Guest House in Hauz Khas, coming in contact with Balanji and through him with you is all part of this design. Our keen desire of finding a divine guide has been ultimately fulfilled. What is most satisfying is that we both were equally attracted towards you and we found in you someone who can take care of our integrated development.

    Ever since you left Delhi, we have been feeling a void which we tried to fulfil by thinking about you and chanting the *mantra* initiated to us. On 16th November (Saturday), I spent about two hours at Balanji's place and listened to one of your past discourses in Delhi. It was very refreshing.

    Coming to certain queries, though by and large things are becoming clearer and clearer, our children's problem still haunts our mind. No doubt that your concern about them has relieved us of our anxiety to a great extent. Still weak moments keep appearing every now and then. We are gradually accepting the reality as far as our elder son Amit is concerned. We are no more very keen to make him an engineer and will be quite happy even if he settles down in some business. As guided by you, we believe that events will unfold themselves in such a way that his problems will be taken care of. However, the lack of interest in studies of our younger son, Rohit, makes us worried quite often. Perhaps we are not able to decide what to do. We pray you to guide us, so as to get rid of this anxiety. We also need guidance as to what is our duty in such a situation. To be open with you, let me admit that this anxiety also makes me at times to lose my temper and subsequently I feel guilty about it. Please take me out of this vicious cycle.

Except this we have no anxiety at the moment. Fortunately my wife and I think alike and we communicate with each other very well. Though it has been a long process, but the process has increased our faith manifold. We feel quite sufficient when it comes to material achievements. We have enough for our personal and social needs. We have sufficient number of good friends and well wishers. My job has given me good name and fame. And by God's grace we are trying to serve the society in our humble way.

We are still in the Guest House and hope to get accommodation soon. Balanji told me that December program in Ashrama exists but we shall not be able to come this time. However, we shall be looking forward to visit the Ashrama at the earliest possible opportunity.

I am studying Srimad Bhagavad Gita regularly and also chanting *mantra*. This gives me peace and makes thinking more clear.

Coming in contact with Aroopji and Deepaji has also been a great pleasure. Our reverence to both of them. We look forward to your reply as early as possible.

Our Pranams to all the inmates of the Ashrama.

Yours humbly
Rakesh Mittal
Aruna Mittal

The reply to this letter came after about a month. I was pleasantly surprised to see a nine-page letter, typed by Swamiji himself. I took it as a sign of the special grace of Swamiji, which not only removed many of our doubts but also recharged us. For the first time I received deep spiritual wisdom from a great master in such simple words. I am reproducing this letter in its original form.

Narayanashrama Tapovanam,
Venginissery, P.O. Paralam, Trichur, Kerala,
India-680575
14th December 1991

Dear and blessed Rakesh and Aruna,

Hari Om Tat Sat. Your letter of 28th November came in time, but I could not write to you earlier. And perhaps it will interest you to know why and how.

I reached back, with Aroop and Deepa on 10th November, though the promised date was 7th. Next day, I went to Vyasa Tapovanam, to see Swami Purushothama Tirtha and tell him about what all took place in Delhi. We usually also discuss the HNP affairs and projects, during such occasions.

And on the 12th started, rather restarted the huge work on the *Pandavagiri* top. Once this happened, your Swamiji was almost on a mountaineering zeal and commitment. As advised by Dr. Dharma Chatterjee of Delhi, Deepa was taken to the doctors, and ultimately the operation was decided on, rather too soon. She perhaps felt that the hospitalization and the additional time-bound measures for the purpose, more important than all her absence from the Ashrama, would normally necessitate the stopping of the hill-top work, where over 75 workers assembled daily by 8 AM. But I felt that the work and hospitalization should both be on, without suffering any inattention.

I promised her to be in the hospital morning and evening. And at 6, I used to be on the backseat of the car, with some others to be left there in the hospital, and with morning coffee and tea. Coming back about 7:40, I changed my dress and ran up the hill, a task, which, when to be done more than once a day, is fatiguing to anyone. The only time I was away was when the workers would stop for their midday meal. I would be in the Ashrama for about an hour, within which I would have to clean myself and take food. Rest scanty.

Before 2 PM again on top, to be retiring for the day at about 5:45 or 6 PM. I did not find enough time or leisure to go around the different points of work and plan for or think. A question I always ask and speak about: "Are we impairing the hill, nature's bounty, or are we preserving and enriching it, for the use of the people and devotees." The answer from all quarters has been, we are doing the latter.

Deepa came back on 2nd, and for rest and convenience has occupied the space available just behind the typewriter on which I write this letter. Usually she stays in a building at a distance which is 24 feet higher. Somehow I have always found and felt that everything is to be done. "If you want to get anything done, go to the busy man", is the celebrated proverb.

With goggles, full sleeve shirt, and now with socks and *chappals*, a stick to ornament my hand and steps, I move up and down the hill-top, climbing up, down, across, slipping, tilting, falling, bending and doing many other features. Several times my body has fallen, and I say, I am a country boy, and not easily would be hurt. My fingertips have been scratched and cut, because I lifted small rough stones to help one person or another, with a sense of irresistible involvement. Yesterday and day before, I could not type because of pain. Today I decided to withstand the touch and am doing this letter.

The Kerala *bandh* people, without any prior notice, came about 10 AM and wished us to stop work. About 60 persons had been working. So these modern, democratic phenomena are not alone for you, but also for us, the ascetics.

At one point, after having said "we request your cooperation for *bandh*", to which I replied "why so late; you could have done this before 8 AM". Some workers resented, perhaps, the request, and the leaders then were in my front, with humility, suggesting that I call the work off. Meanwhile, one said, "in any case, we would not allow the work." I sternly then said: "Why this uncalled for discourteous statement? On one hand you seek cooperation, and right thereafter, you use the language of force. Democracy does not allow the creed of violence or physical force. The *hita* of people has to be raised in favour of or against any objective. *Jana-hita* is democracy. I had not brought even the attendance register. Those who wanted to honour the *bandh* call, I had felt and said would not come for work and need not. But those who wanted to work, could do so. Distant workers, I had specifically said, not to come. You did not tell me either last evening or this morning that your *bandh* is also a request before me..."

Anyway, so many men and women, belonging to their political factions came for work. That itself proves against them.

One unique point is that I wanted to write to you on this letterhead. But the stock was over and the printer had not delivered the new set. I was almost to take the HNP one, but somehow turned back more than once. In this way, this letter carries a distinction.

Now, to come to your letter and its contents:

Yes, it is indeed a rare fortune, to be under the care of *Sajjana*. *Shankara* describes three rare bounties of human life: *Manushyatvum, Mumukshutvam, Mahaapurusha-samsrayah.*

The third word means: faithful dependence on and care from a *Mahapurusha*.

The creation is vast, beautiful, imposing, and multiply alluring. All get drawn to its Majesty and Splendour, and become busy in enjoying the gift. It does not easily occur to anyone: "How has all this come about and who should be behind this spread out affluence. If this, His product, is so alluring, how much more infinitely should be He, Himself?"

Dear souls, if at any time such a unique thought takes over one's mind that is the beginning of an immortal fortune. But, in some cases, despite such an august note, the beneficiary will be surrounded by the usual and common, or even the unusual and uncommon adversities and seeming disharmonies.

Bring to mind, *Prahlada*, the chosen devotee of Lord Hari. See how squarely he had to differ from his powerful

Emperor father and how the confrontation led to the father shedding all his paternal bonds, and rising in stark enmity and cruelty against the small 7-year old boy. He engaged several demons to try to liquidate the son. Some to administer poison through food, some to pierce in his tender stomach, some to drop huge rocks on his head, some to get serpents bite him, and yet some endeavour in many more ways.

And what was the cause? The tender boy enjoyed the invisible grace his heart generated and bestowed upon. Such freedom does not encroach upon any individual. But the choice of the heart is much strong than the will of the muscle.

Should a chosen devotee of the Lord be processed through such heart-rending environments and episodes? But it happened. Are not at least a few such repetitive instances in the world of mankind vis-a-vis devotion and self-realization? It is wrong to think or say that "O, it was Prahlada; and what am I; not he, anyone near..."

If you are one among these few and I believe and find this is this is this so quite possibly some adversities may visit you. You have to take your parental fate as merely that. The great gain and the most tremendous loss, both, mind you, are in the perishable world, and of the perishables. The pleasure visiting one and the pain intruding into his life, both are of and from the perishable world. Like zero, this perishability, is the final multiplication figure, to all the numbers and quantities of world fortune and misfortune alike. Do you get the point? Is it clear?

The life term is temporary. And in this temporariness the only great factor is that during its tenure the human can elevate himself to the permanent status. That comes from the Soul, which is not the body at all. Boyhood, youth, parenthood and what else not; all relate to the body. The ornamentation or ugliness relating to the body, becomes a simple "nil factor" when you look to the soul which is fully un-body, non-body.

Either through simple and fortunate developments, people should turn to the soul, the permanent factor, and through complex and unfortunate situations, the compulsion should take place. I am not saying that you are to be reckoned as among the second group. But I do say that you are one noble seeker devotee like Prahlada or Dhruva. Percentages may differ, as in a class examination or even in administrative selectees.

In such a thorough background, fundamental and deeply pious, look at your role as parents. We have no choice in the matter of our own birth; likewise, we have no choice in the matter of our children's birth. Now, birth itself can be avoided or delayed, medicine says. But the nature of the embryo, its growth, its outer and inner features, when born, are all subject to as much as favourableness as to unfavourableness. And the *nirdwandwa* attitude is what is truly called for. If healthy and well-behaved children, with intelligence are born, then we shall look after them and leave them to be useful to the world. If not so, then we shall undertake the loyal austere pilgrimage of tending them even more heartily and with the sense of piety, and do maximum to ensure their welfare, to the point till we ourselves leave our bodies.

Sraddha is generally performed till one's own demise to the parents. Two points are important here: the children go on doing *Sraddha* for parents alone, and whether the parents themselves would have been reborn, if at all, even while the children continue to do *Sraddha* for decades, is a full uncertainty. Again, the ceremonial offer and discipline takes place only as long as the children themselves live. Is it not then self-based and self-judged? This is the principle in trying to tend the children and their welfare. What would follow, after the parents themselves leave the world, is as much in the hands of chance and uncertainty as those of the Great Creator.

Reflect upon the first parentage, and the very human institution itself. Were not the first humans shaped and reared by the Creator, about whom no insufficiency or incompetence can be adduced. Having descended from Him, why so much of complainable and notorious traits, both physical and mental, in His children-series? How does He take the fate or plight, and what is His consolation or redress?

You and others have become parents much, much later in time and series. Is not the thought and ego then an intrusion, truly?

I think in the ultimate view, either everything belongs to us, in our life, or nothing does. Just like you find usefulness and blessings in living in the transit accommodation, you can find usefulness and timely beneficialness in whatever visits and thrusts upon your life, be it the birth of children, their fate, or a position in administration, or what not.

Generally, prosperity is one blessing (*Abhyudaya*) and *Nishreyasa* is the other. When *Nishreyasa* is begun to be sought, then you will find that the incumbent gets, is driven to whatever will help this fortune.

There is one Srimati Nalini Baliga, who once came to me in the same room in which you sat with me inside. One after another, two children came in, with suspicious gaits and approaches. She gracefully spoke to them in their language, dissuaded them. Both, woefully were retarded. Out of the few sentences she spoke to me, one, somewhat I shall reproduce: "Swamiji, I find enough fulfilment in looking after these children. My devotion to God makes me feel that this is his *prasada*. The plight makes me more and more sublime, warm and considerate. It is a blessing..." One of the two, possibly, is no more now, if my memory is correct.

So at any time let not your minds think adversely about the seeming adverse plight you as parents, find yourself in. You are parents as God and Goddesses are, before mankind. Reflect upon this higher magnitude, whenever the lower ones, the terrestrial ones, parade your mind. And see what happens.

But my heart and mind remember lovingly and sweetly about the sons, and they will continue to feel so. You will find me share your lot in this. Enough is already in what I have written, as answer to your question: 'what is our duty in such instances?'

There is no duty: there is only a natural role, response and reaction. Role and response need not be elaborated upon. Reaction is subject to evaluation, culture, refinement and progression. And I have done this for you, I think.

When the minds of you both become more and more sublime, and the great sense and note of impersonality, impartiality and neutrality begins to dawn and grace the mind, that beginning is itself the best treasure and source, by which the most corrective and sublime influences will emerge and work on the plight.

As heat radiates from fire, brilliance from lamp, the most auspicious rays radiate from our mind, when it is sublime, good, serene and pure. Object-wise, it is perhaps a discouraging or enervating situation — no I do not like to say this. But subject-wise it is quite helpful and rewarding.

What any parent would derive in the presence of healthy and intelligent children, more than that a felicity far greater and long-standing in dimension and depth, you parents will derive. Be sure.

Let me know from time to time what the situation is about the children. Tell them fondly that there is a Swami who thinks of them very-very fondly.

About irritation, I think you should set a time limit, for sublimating it. When a trouble confronts it is first judged and felt, in notes of intolerance or irritation. Irritation with a person or group, is bad, we say. But when a thorn enters the foot, should not the foot feel irritated. In fact it is such pain and irritation that leads the system to bring it out.

Beyond this, irritability is an unwelcome trait. Knowing that it is not an ornament, is a first step in correction. The next step lies in changing or upgrading our response to it. In developing a sympathetic note, and adjusting and reconciling note, is this upgradation. The world around is meant to produce a number of responses and reactions, each of which is sublimating and fulfilling to the human mind. As is love so is hatred. As is attachment so too is detachment. As is preference so too is prejudice. Similarly, love, sympathy, sacrifice are, which are the basic and ultimate emotions to grace and complete the mind. Have more and more of sympathy, love and take every occasion to get enriched by sacrifice. Perhaps the children would evoke and call for these, more than will any individual outside.

This new outlook, if at all it is so, should take say a year, to be stabilized. Meanwhile, or even later, a few eruptions might occur. Do not be bothered. Accept them, as also part of creation, not, of course, to indulge in them more freely, but to rise above them.

See, here, on the hill top, moving up and down, here and there with the workers, this Swami is now a Master, of whom all, of a lot consisting of almost a full variety. He has to speak words and show moods, naturally enough, which he would not like to display or possess, but which he is led to be in the midst of. He does it as a sport. Out of the 60 or more workers, men and women, some are willing, more so, some inexperienced, some reluctant to do heavier or difficult jobs. He tells them:

We are not working here with or by force. I only want you to do that much which you can, well and easily. The task itself is huge, tremendous, and burdensome. And you alone are going to accomplish. By sparing any item, in fact, none stands to gain. At the same time, let each of you turn to or away from specific difficulties, depending upon his or her ability. We have enough persons, to substitute anyone. Do not link the remuneration you get with the work you do. Money is a need and a little of that is being given. For the sincerity and devotion of a worker, there cannot be a monetary reward.

Sometimes, they make references to 'Swamiji will scold'. I say, do not say that. I scold none, and I dislike none. Anyone who is weak or fatigued can take rest. Otherwise, each should work well. As am I, so are you all, in this project.

Irritations do become part of such a colossal venture. I would always be happier in the midst of enlightened or cultured devotees. Often, I have to be with non-devotees also. With heretics and rationalists, in halls and public places, which are like the fish and flesh markets to my mind. But thinking of the purpose for which they get me, I conduct myself, with felicity and come away.

I do not expect Nature or her Lord to surround me with everything that is nice. I only wish and intend that what our country and its standards, they alone would I also have, and need. Let me not have excellent health, but only reasonably, tolerable health.

The Asramhold is a far bigger household. The expenditure we have to bear, on so many fronts mount and frighten also. I always say that to incur X minus 1 after getting X, is the way of business. Industrialists plan in such a way. For the ascetic framework, it is always the reverse. X plus 1 will be made to be spent, and against that scanty X will visit. My heart emphasizes and delights in this process. I discuss with Purushothama Swamiji the points, and we find safety in going ahead with whatever huge projects we are on.

In everything, the love for the people at large, their eternal though often unfelt needs, the country Bharat, Her legacy, the need to perpetuate it, live in us.

From 1984 HNP, the registered trust with *Sanyasins* as Trustees, took up the religious and spiritual revivalist movements, and old age homes, helping the villagers, helpless aged, giving help of other kinds for treatment, house building etc., came in. Also a few dilapidated temples were taken over for setting matters right, so that worship would go on. Lands in the name of temple were taken over by the Government and this rendered temples orphans almost.

The *Pandavagiri* Shrine and work on reclamation, restoration of the *Giri* and rebuilding and building the shrine complex stands as huge and very important, more age-old then all else. Somehow our ashrama being on its slope, and our Mataji, Sulbha Devi, whose *Samadhi Day* falls on 25th December, was fondly telling me several times; "Father, something should be done for the Temple. It is not right that we live here down, and the shrine is left to languish..." My reply was: "Temple is a running institution, with its legends and legacies. To think of entering the area would be to take up a big responsibility. And for us *Sanyasins*, it would be disharmonious. If and when the local people and management want us to help in any way, I shall..."

Such a help, not much, was earlier sought and given. But the languishing continued, until at last some years ago, a theft intercepted the daily worship, and an astrological consultation became necessary, in which the wrongs and remedial measures in the worship and other rituals were pinpointed. A five-day purificatory ritual was ordered. For its conduct, I lent support, primarily by my presence and addresses to devotees, on whom by the last day I thrust two commitments: "To do a *Nama Sankirtan, Giri pradakshina*, in which finally over 1500 people participated, and then to undertake a *Pratijna* that we, the present generation, would not disprove the trust reposed on us by ancestors. We would strive to preserve the place, its sanctity, and age old memories and associations. The entire hilltop and surroundings would be cared for, preserved and made into what the first builder Lord *Parasurama* in *Treta Yuga* and what later, *Draupadi* and *Pandavas* who camped there during their *Vanvaasa*, and on whom special blessings for success as well as inseparable marital bonds, were granted.

Perhaps this *Pratijna* made by them, was in truth a commitment, as it was for Krishna, who clearly stipulated "I would not wield weapons or participate directly in war", before agreeing to accept the choice of Arjuna: "Between your big army and yourself I choose you alone, single- personally". The topsy-turvy development resulted in the people, the government, *Cochin Devaswam* Board together entrusting the management to HNP. Clearing the loans incurred by the impoverished local management committee, making additional appointments and instituting a system for daily running of the worship, we began our participation, like Krishna, and nominated a committee to handle the affairs. Even now, though born in temples and grown there, largely,

I do not delight in visiting Temples. But I do speak for them and explain and strengthen their purpose, place and role. The Hindu society has never made memorials for "wives or even parents". But its members have spent huge and appalling amounts, greater than our present five year plan outlays, in bringing up worship places and Pilgrim Centres. In fact, for any village or even township, the only long-living identity at least in South India is the existence of such shrines, which are like Mind Health Centres and Hospitals, and parks at least.

Our country has yet to recognize the greatly rural structure of our population and civilization. And in such a context these places and institutions have all the more importance and relevance.

To participate or help in building, preserving, restoring or renovating any place of pilgrimage or shrine is an incalculable fortune.

Dear Rakesh and Aruna, it was my wish that before the reconstruction matters are over, the temple must have its courtyard, outer *praakaara*, where devotees can conveniently do *pradakshina*.

This meant carrying earth head load, a work that bulldozers cannot do, I was told. We have raised one-half, almost of this *praakaara*. The heights achieved maximum on this southern side is 25 feet or more. On the other half, northern, it is even more. A circular road is also to be made, which too has been more than half. The final steps to get to the temple ground will be 27 on the west front and 9 on the east, the other front.

Every week, the work calls Rs. 20,000 for wages alone. Materials are aside. Over 100 truck loads have already gone into raising the rubble masonry retaining wall. The courtyard *praakaara* when raised, would be 22 ft/180 ft. On the eastern front, looking on *Sahyadri*, the place gives a beautiful sunrise sight, which is rare. On the back of the temple is the Arabian sea, and backwater areas. I would like as many people as possible to visit the place and feast their eyes and nourish the heart.

Many already come and the work has led to even more to come in.

I would like as many of our devotees as possible to participate in this grandeur, primarily because such great ventures must be done as a *Satra*, sharing in from many. Secondly, it is immensely rewarding and blessing to play at least the squirrel's role in the unique *Setu Bandhana*. I don't know of your interests, maybe, you will find some interest and a personal touch too.

Personal fondness, fondness of a personal nature, is the greatest moving force on earth. Guru-love or *Bhakti*, is also, perhaps the most top ranking in this. Is *Guru Bhakti* greater or *Sishya Prema*? God descends and even humiliates Himself, when so called and needed by devotees, who develops personal love for Him.

In the case of your Swami he is *Nishkinchana*, an *akinchana*, to the core. But, for the sake of personal notes, related to his devotees, he has moved earth, heaven and hell often. For me, God was a closed chapter decades back. And devotees are the continuing chapter. Thoughts about them, including those for Mataji, are what make me move up the hill and get scorched. It is an austerity, and such austerity alone must go to make shrines.

We have spent over 6 or 7 lakhs of rupees so far, and the whole work including a bore well, quarters, urinals, etc., with some additional temple facilities, primarily educational and enlightening in character, will cost anything around 20 lacs. A small village here or there cannot handle the task at all. The astrological assembly, which is the guiding factor for all these affairs, held that the place has ascetic background and source, and caves of *Tapasvins* can even be spotted by them astrologically now. An ascetic has to head the matters even now, and that is perhaps how a Swami has come over.

When over 27 years back I looked for a place, like Shri Ram, to setup my hermitage, I wanted specifically an area or place where none had inhabited. And came naturally or providentially to this *Tapovanam* area. Later, on arrival, I heard all the story of *Pandavagiri*.

O.K. It is the third morning, since I began to write on the typewriter, which goes on overlapping while typing: I don't know when I wrote such a long letter, and whether you will like it too. At least let it be a monument of my fondness for you, and concern for your children.

You have pinned on Self realization. Be sure, and clear, that once this becomes your ideal, there is or will be nothing in your life's course, over which you have any ground or cause to grieve, shall I say unduly. Whether it is children, or a place to do officing or otherwise.

Before a clear and devout mind, even rocks would melt. The sea would split, and mountains suddenly go down.

Nothing should or will surprise, nor anything enchant beyond measure.

As are so many, so are our children. As are other parents so are we. Remember God, the only and first and last parent. Remember the beloved Lord, who is as well the most nourishing son.

Take your position alternately, personally and impersonally, partially and impartially as the occasion compels, and be sooner or later, delight in the basic neutrality and temporality of life.

Not only the earth has descended from supreme heights, the human soul thriving in it with a body has come down from still greater heights. And, naturally, surely, and also as choice and a welcome outcome, the soul has to go back, as Rama and Krishna.

Rakesh and Aruna are also alike, maybe differently and perhaps in a smaller measure, if you like to think so.

Love and *Ashirwad*

Yours Swamiji

P.S. Let me rush up, with my finger like stick, socks and chappals, to be slipping often in the dishevelled lap of the great goddess.

A letter like this needs repeated readings to be grasped properly. Swamiji himself mentioned that he hardly ever wrote such long letters and it was a monument of his fondness for us. It was absolutely true because this letter totally changed our perception of the situation and we started seeing blessings in all events of life. Obviously it did not happen in a day; Swamiji himself indicated a time limit of about a year for sublimation of our trouble and we found it reasonable.

I would also like to mention that the contents of this letter show the multidimensional personality of Swamiji and gives the message that a spiritual person is also a worldly person. The description of his working in the ashrama reminds me of the working of Mahatama Gandhi in his South Africa or Sabarmati ashramas where all serious political matters were managed while engaged in daily mundane activities. In case of Swamiji, the matters are spiritual and social.

In my next letter to Swamiji written on January 14, 1992, I responded to the above letter after deep contemplation. Every time I read this letter tears roll down my eyes even now. These tears make me even stronger to face the vicissitudes of life in whatever field they are. This letter goes like this:

> K-114 Hauz Khas,
> New Delhi – 110016
> 14.1.1992
>
> Our most revered Swamiji,
> Pranams,
>
> We have no words to express our pleasure on receipt of your illuminating letter. We really take it as a monument of your fondness and concern for us. It has given us lot of guidance, clarified our doubts and will continue to do so. The fact that you took so much time off from your busy schedule and typed the letter yourself adds further to our pleasure. I am sure you will continue to bestow your blessings on us.
>
> Every word of your letter has a message for us. Gradually we shall absorb it and also adopt. There is no

disagreement with any part of it. We assure you that we shall take our environment, the way you have pointed out. We really don't know whether we fall in the category of Dhruva or Prahlada, but we certainly derive strength from this comparison. Already we have started feeling that the incidents around us are leading us to fulfilment. Hopefully the process will continue till self realization is reached. Mind is becoming more and more clear and purposeful.

Your comparison of perishability as final multiplication by zero, is very revealing. So is the limited utility of irritability. This will greatly help in stabilizing the mind within the time limit indicated by you. The endeavour would be to reduce it further. We greatly count on your blessings in this regard.

Coming to certain mundane developments in the intervening period, two things are important. Firstly the house allotment process has been quite painful (it has not been allotted till today). After you left Delhi, we were expecting allotment any day. I was trying to take the assistance of my Minister, but by coincidence the additional PS of the Housing Minister promised allotment in exchange of some help to his friend. However that fellow made me to run like anything and ultimately got me allotted a house, which has already been allotted. Then another house was allotted which was to be vacated but the occupant changed his mind. So at present, the position is back to square one. I met the Secretary several times but no help came. I am writing to you all this because it has been an experience of life for me. Fortunately it has stopped bothering me now and in the process we have learnt several lessons, which shall be of immense benefits to us in future. As I mentioned in my earlier letter that living in transit accommodation has its own usefulness and so I have now left things to take their own course. The second matter is about my elder son, Amit. He was shown to another doctor, who has returned from USA, and has good exposure in the field of neurology. After investigation, he has concluded the problem is 'Genetic Mypathy'. He has advised no further investigation and also suggested no cure except some supportive measures. He has advised tendon lengthening surgery for both Amit and Rohit, in order to prolong muscular degeneration. However we have decided not to go for it in near future. Meanwhile one close relative of ours and an amateur Homeopath has claimed near treatment of the disease. We are exploring all the possibilities in this regard. Other sciences of treatment are also being explored. If you have to suggest anything in this regard please do.

Fortunately Aruna's faith is intact. She is becoming more and more devoted in her cause. I too feel that all this has a purpose in our lives and there is no feeling of complaint or bitterness. We are now much more prepared to accept the reality than was the case sometime back. It is making us more and more sublime and concerned for all those who suffer.

We have noted with great interest, the development of Pandav Giri hills under your supervision. We long to visit the place at the earliest possible. The intention is to visit during Guru Purnima, if nothing goes otherwise we would like to bring Amit and Rohit also. Could exact dates be indicated now?

We fully agree with your views on the reconstruction work and we are all for it. Whatever little we can do for this cause, will give us immense pleasure. Similar reconstruction is required everywhere and in all walks of life.

A few words about the New Year's Eve. We spent it with Balan ji and his wife at our guest house. We ate together and talked about you. He also went through your letter. We really had a nice time.

We are not able to attend all the Satsangs, due to various reasons but we wish to. Let us hope that we shall be able to do so, after settling down in regular accommodation.

I want to send life subscription for 'Vicher Sethu', please send details. Aroopji and Deepaji must be fine. Our deep regards to them and all inmates of Ashrama.

Our pranams to you again.

Yours Humbly
Rakesh Mittal

Aruna Mittal.

Before I got the reply of this letter, I wrote another letter on February 5, 1992 informing Swamiji about my house allotment. Swamiji acknowledged both and gave his response in his letter dated February 11, 1992. This letter, again, was very inspiring and added to my clarity, and confirmed the way I proposed to proceed. This letter of Swamiji is reproduced below.

Narayanashrama Tapovanam,
Venginissery, P.O. Paralam, Trichur,
Kerala, India-680575
11th February 1992

Dear and blessed Rakesh and Aruna:
Hari Om Tat Sat.

Your letter of 5th and earlier one also to hand. All the thoughts, sentiments and notes of piety and seeking you had written make very good reading, and they have touched my heart. Let the grace and sublimity which they deserve bless you in ample measure.

The offering you have sent for the *Pandava Giri Durga* temple and the *Pandavagiri* restoration cause is heartily acknowledged. I am sending the DD to Shri Swami Purushottama Tirth Ji, Vyasa Tapovanam, for entering into the HNP books, and issuing the necessary receipt. Possibly the receipt will also accompany this letter. This should suffice for IT relief you have in mind.

The work proves to be even more stupendous as it progresses. I wanted to stop work on Saturday last, 8th and declared also accordingly. But some unfinished portions had to be attended to, specially, and so it has continued up to the time of writing this letter.

It is good that you have also shared in the striving. Tomorrow, I am leaving for Jamshedpur, via Madras, Calcutta, and Aroop and Deepa will accompany me. Their homes are in Calcutta and JSR. We would be back on 14th

March. The weeks to follow are rather indefinite, because of the Kondungallur Devi Temple Aswati Pollution Festival falling on April 4th. This practice, accompanied by obscenity singing and using lower community people to ceremonially pollute the temple, after keeping the temple and shrine doors closed, smacks of great degeneration and abuse, both in field of devotion and that of social cohesion and respect. We have been moving for correction and updating of the practices for the past 4 years. This year our move is almost resolved to be Akhand Upavasa in the Temple itself, which is not going to be easy either to conduct or to be enabled and tolerated by the administration as well as the opponents. But some more details have to be worked out before actually announcing the move in the Press. My absence immediately before the crucial period makes things harder also.

I am happy that you have been allotted a house, which also pleases your hearts. Very good. The right note with regard to a person like you is: One always gets what one rightly deserves, one's nature rightly deserves. This means that whatever is got is that which one has rightly deserved. How each development conforms to this basic law, is a point which has to be properly assessed and appreciated each time. So the thinking should actually be on this aspect.

Meanwhile, even if you had approached someone for courtesy or attention, it does not matter. Such events take away one's ego and make him soft. To have no ego, and yet to have right ego, is both a riddle and contradiction. To resolve this and to be in harmony with such continuing contradictions is in a way, the true spiritual sublimity.

The Mahabharata war was approaching. Yudhistira's mind got restless, thinking about the consequences. The huge bloodshed frightened and depressed him. He conversed with the brothers and Krishna. Krishna was always a special benefactor to him. He said: "Dear Krishna, I am extremely afflicted. I want someone to go to Duryodhana and talk to him for truce. The object must be to avoid bloodshed at any cost. Who can achieve this except you? I consider you best for the purpose..."

Krishna spoke back: "My dear brother, the welfare of your mind is my constant concern. And to ensure this, whatever is needed I shall do. Knowing as I do Duryodhana's mind, I feel he will not listen to any truce proposals. He is one who has no regard for the society or dharma. And by being so, he does not feel the least pang or discomfort. Of what use then will it be to talk to him, gospels of peace and coexistence? Yet, to please you and appease your heart, I shall myself undertake the mission of an ambassador. I shall speak to him using the best of words and adopting the most moving sentiments and styles..."

What do you notice in this? Was not Krishna ready and willing to do something which he clearly knew, was disharmonious and unnecessary? To attempt a task successful and praise worthy, even the most lazy soul will come forth. To take a mission, which is likely to be fruitless and even hazardous, even the most intelligent will not be so ready. But the course of sublimity to crown the human mind is entirely different.

Gandhari, at the end of the war happened to open her eyes, the last time in her life, to see the treachery of Kurukshetra. And then she turned to Krishna to say: "Krishna you are the sole cause for this entire tragedy. Mind you, your clan also will be destroyed similarly...."

Krishna smiled, obviously greeting the pronouncement with cheerful impartiality and indifference.

In such great contexts, I think you have only stood to be graced with sublimity, in whatever has preceded your being allotted the house. Of course, the pivot is the manner in which you view the whole series of actions and effects.

Ok let me stop. Love and Sivasis.

I remember the children, and let them go ahead with their own heartiness and fullness. They should be sure about the propriety and sincerity of what they do and strive for. Make them responsible this way.

Loving blessings to them also.

Yours
Swamiji

This was my limited correspondence with Swamiji as far as his spiritual guidance was concerned. These two letters of Swamiji set our spiritual agenda to a great extent and thereafter we only shared minor personal matters to which his responses were quick and clear. Even in administrative field he gave me many pieces of advice from time to time which facilitated me to handle various situations in a harmonious manner. In this continuation I shall reproduce two more letters—one by me of August 4, 1992 and its reply on August 16, 1992. My letter was written soon after we received the first *Guru Poornima* blessings in which I mentioned some problems in the domestic front. It goes as:

O-2-1 MS Flats,
R. K. Puram Sector 13
New Delhi – 110066
4.8.1992

Rev. Swamiji,
Pranams.

We are delighted to receive your blessings on the auspicious occasion of *Guru Poornima*. Though we missed the occasion, we hope it will be better planned in near future. In retrospect, I feel that the programme as worked out in June could have been stuck to. Anyway it was to be so. 'Vichar Setu' has started reaching us regularly and we have received April, May, June issues. Write up of Deepaji is very inspiring.

Noted your advice about the change of exercise from play to plain walking. I am doing the same at present. I also feel it to be more conducive from spiritual viewpoint. However giving up tennis altogether is appearing difficult at the moment. I had decided to keep away for two months. Please guide.

Things are going well at home front. We have lot of guests in Delhi and sometimes it disturbs our tranquillity. At that time we feel bad but don't know what to do. By nature we welcome guests and take their due care. It also puts lot of pressure on Aruna, who has only limited domestic help. She does not want to miss her Pooja/Japa schedule and she does so at the cost of her sleep, resulting in physical troubles like headache, depression, etc. We have been facing this problem for some time and need your guidance in the matter.

Amit and Rohit are fine. Amit has appeared in the 1st semester examination of B. Com. and has done well. He is now doing second semester, though the result is awaited. He is also joining a computer course from 8/8/92. This way his schedule is full. He is now showing interest in studies and hopefully will do well. We are working hard on the younger one Rohit, though at times his studies upset us. He has not as yet started feeling responsible and in competitive environment like Delhi, it becomes difficult for us not to compare him with others, fully knowing it is not fair to do so.

Regarding treatment of Amit, both Homeopathy and Unani is going on. There is marginal improvement; at least there is no deterioration. However we are satisfied in the sense that all possible attention is being paid.

We have bothered you with too many of our problems but who else can give us the proper direction. At least we feel unburdened by doing so. I was waiting for Balanji to return but there are still some days left. We shall learn more about the ashrama on his return. We are also looking forward with eagerness to your visit to Delhi in the month of October. Hopefully the dates must have been finalized by now.

Rest is fine.

Aruna, Amit and Rohit convey their pranams to you. Pranams to Aroop ji and Deepaji.
Pranams again.

Yours Humbly,
Rakesh

Narayanashrama Tapovanam,
Venginissery, P.O. Paralam, Trichur,
Kerala, India-680575
16th August 1992

Dear and blessed Rakesh and Aruna:
Hari Om Tat Sat

Your letter of 4th to hand. I note the points you have related. Any habit is steadily acquired and if at all left also steadily. Steady leaving must be possible. Let tennis leaving also in its own manner be a significant discipline, *sadhana*, for you. The art of cultivating a habit also lends itself to outliving it.

About guests being welcome and this devotion interfering with the Godly devotion: It is always nice to be good, gentle and amiable to others. Such qualities, by their very nature, will bring in others nearby. In fact, amiableness lends itself to such freedom and proximity. But not many of those who come closely will be equally amiable and sensitive. Often emotional excellence is not followed by intelligential sensitiveness. This is a chronic disorder, disharmony, with humans, especially with the so-called devotees. How to deal with the situation?

If Aruna takes the very loving service and hospitality extended to guests as her devotional pursuit and *sadhana* and does not think that *Pooja* routines disabled on such occasions pose a problem, one part of the confrontation and torment will be over. But the other part will remain. Guests will continue to come, as long as her hospitality is warm and hearty. Is it possible to regulate arrival of guests, as if water from a tap? A measure of conflict and trouble will continue.

But, for health reasons, she has to take a more personal and objective view. Whenever possible, let the difficulties be made known to those intending to come. Also, let a new note of making those who come sharing her domestic burdens be incorporated in her habits.

Another distinct note she must be clear about is that she should make the guests know warmly that she keeps to some religious routines, and it is desirable that the guests also make it convenient by all kinds of sharing and adjustment. The options will be then clear: either those who come will heartily take to the *pooja* routines, being present then, or prefer not to be disturbed and disturb. That will be a kind of filtering. I think it is better allowed earlier than later. Within Delhi, she must always make her friends know that a specific duration is kept for her piety, and during then others should heartily cooperate by not wanting her time and attention.

I think privacy is something that all gentleman and gentlewomen must appreciate and adjust themselves to, although in Indian context this is something widely lacking. *Spiritual Sadhana* is beyond a point more and more behavioural than otherwise.

About the children, I am happy that some hopeful notes are there. Let us strive consistently. The *mantra* I had given them must be resorted to with even more wholesomeness and dedication. It will be effective considerably. Whatever medical care and exercise are necessary, they should also be provided.

There was a report in the papers about a Tamil child taken to a doctor as he was not speaking as usual at the usual age. The doctor gave the parents a cassette of 90 minutes on *Shiv Puranam*, asking to play it repeatedly to the child. The boy has turned to be a prodigy, able to recite hundreds of *Thirukkaralgrantha*, a classical composition. He has been admitted straight away to the third class after finding his Intelligence quotient.

The maker of the body is the power that rules its organs and also causes diseases. If one can invoke the spirit's power, diseases can also be cured. But this is an empirical science, and so cannot be tested, verified and repeated in pursuit. Hence we say it is providential.

Providence generally favours those who seek it and rely on its Power.

Homoeopathic medicines can act wonderfully, when rightly identified. Maybe the symptoms of this disorder are not unknown to its science. Unani, if faithfully practiced by the practitioner must also be good. Some reservation I feel about how well the practitioners handle it.

Balan Ji must have returned by the time this letter arrives and he must have briefed you all the news here. Together with Nirupamananda, I would proceed for Muscat on 2nd, and return to Ashrama On 18th, and in a few days will have to start for Delhi. This time we are inaugurating our stay and life in the Ashrama at Deoli. The programs at Delhi must be helped and strengthened by all devotees and seekers, especially in our group.

Human mind has many noble and elevating sentiments and attitudes. *Upeksha* or indifference is one of these. In all matters, one generally grows ego, desire and greed, possessiveness and the like. Equally so, later, in a more mature state egolessness, desire absence and non-possessiveness must be the style and goal. Geeta speaks about these in the 13th chapter, commencing from *AManitvam*.... It is possible to have these subtle embellishments. Keep this point in mind, and help and allow the qualities to enrich your thoughts and moves.

Love and *sivasis* to you both, love and blessings to children.

Yours
Swamiji

This letter of Swamiji further clarified our doubts. Thereafter, our correspondence was mainly on routine matters. We were now working on the agenda set by Swamiji's guidance. We were slowly rising above our personal problems, while trying to do our best to take care of them. Narayanashrama Tapovanam's monthly publication *Vichar Setu* was also very helpful in clarifying our doubts which arose from time to time. The letters of devotees to Swamiji and their replies were of particular help.

Early Correspondence with Swamiji

It was now time for Swamiji to arrive in Delhi again and we were eagerly looking for the same. We were well settled by this time and requested the local organizers to fix up a visit of Swamiji at our place also, which was accepted.

Swamiji paid his first visit to our home on November 2, 1992, in the evening. This was on the eve of our completing one year of initiation. We invited many friends and relatives on this occasion. Everyone was deeply influenced by Swamiji and we felt highly blessed by his visit. That year Swamiji did not stay with Balanji but stayed in a farmhouse at Deoli owned by one of his disciples. It was about 18 kilometres from our residence in R. K. Puram. The path to the farmhouse was also not very convenient, which made Swamiiji's schedule even more hectic. We spent several evenings with Swamiji.

By this time Aroopji and Deepa ji had taken full *Sanyasa Diksha* under the name Swami Nirviseshananda (also affectionately called Nutan Swamiji) and Ma Gurupriya. They were now in saffron clothes and displayed powerful radiance. We were greatly benefited by their association also.

This time we hardly discussed our personal problems, though they surfaced from time to time. Swamiji's guidance in handling them was constantly in our mind and we were trying to follow the same. For the first time we realized the impact of being in a holy company. Before long this association became a family bond in which there was hardly any a formality or distance. This only increased our reverence to Swamiji, Nutan Swamiji and Ma Gurupriya.

They stayed in Delhi for about a month and soon the date of their departure arrived. We felt very sad at this moment but what could be done, separation is a necessary part of life. I and Aruna conveyed our feelings to Ma Gurupriya about this association to which she gave a very affectionate reply. Aruna, in particular, was helped by this reply and became more steady in her *Sadhana*.

This letter of Ma goes like this:

Narayanashrama Tapovanam,
Venginissery, P.O. Paralam, Trichur,
Kerala, India-680575
2nd January 1993

"What is spiritual vision in the end? To love and live in this world, FINDING IT GOD, the most beautiful. In this beauty, ugliness will dance, cruelty will sing, compassion and grace will play their notes too. But Indifference must reign. In that the mind is touched, sublimated and refined. The serene content is brought forth well. It is a culture."

Swamiji.

Dear and blessed Aruna,

Hari Om Tat Sat. Your letter of 7th December was received on the 11th. Strangely enough, before receiving your letter, for a few days, quite frequently you were in my thoughts and I myself felt like writing to you. I was remembering those few moments when we were sitting in Swamiji's room one morning; I was also remembering your delightful face while we were in your house. Your face, I do not know why, was bringing a wave of emotion in the mind — love and best wishes were emerging forth from my heart and were surrounding you, your husband and children. Let my Lord's grace be with you always to keep you smiling, contented and to have absolute faith in His love.

By this time Amit's foot must have healed. Did you consult any homeopath? Please let us know about him. I pray to lord that the children may have good health.

We will be leaving for Jamshedpur *Jnana Yajna* on 29th January, returning here after about a month. Things here are going on. Swamiji is very busy with the work in the hilltop. He has become quiet dark being exposed to the sun throughout the day. He comes back very tired and is not able to sit for replying letters.

You might have come to know that I had been to an orthopaedic surgeon soon after I returned from Delhi. By his treatment I am much better now and walk about quite freely. I am still on a reduced dose of vitamins, diet control and exercises. As I was taking medicines suggested by the doctor, I did not try the 'R' compound, which was given by you with much love and concern. I can use them later, if necessary.

Dear Aruna, I was very happy to read your warm and hearty letter which gives a touch of your simplicity. Do not hesitate to write whenever you want and whatever you like. Like a daughter does to a mother, pour out everything what your heart wants to — significant as well as insignificant.

Amit and Rohit's exams must have been over. How have they fared? This letter is as well as to Mittalji, who is very close to our heart. Let your family be graced with happiness and peace in abundant measure.

How is your health? Mittalji's?

With love fondness and blessings
Ma

P.S. Mittalji's letters to Nirviseshananda Ji and Swamiji have been received. The cassette is with us. Shri and Smt. Kamath had to cancel their visit. Maybe we can send with Balan uncle when they come in January.

Dear and blessed Mittal ji,
Hari Om Tat Sat. This morning (5th January) Swamiji asked me to write to you. Swamiji feels that during our next trip to Delhi in April, it will be better if you arrange for his lecture in one place outside Delhi. Many places, as have been suggested by you will not be alright.

Since 17th November Swamiji is fully involved with the temple work and hardly rests. Swamiji said he would send you the blessings for your book conveniently.

Hope everything there is ok and that you are able to spend more time for your spiritual and devotional routines.

With love and blessings
Ma

My reply to this letter is also important as it had further guided us in our future *sadhana*. The letter goes like this.

O-2-1 R. K. Puram, Sector 13
New Delhi – 110066
14/1/ 93

Rev. Ma Gurupriya,
Pranam.

We are delighted to receive your very affectionate letter day before yesterday. In fact we have been eagerly waiting for the same. The delay is very well understood by us. Swamiji has to attend to so many tasks and also to so many devotees. However it gives us immense pleasure that all of you keep us in mind so fondly and pray for Lord's grace. What else a devotee needs?

Aruna is particularly very happy to note your grace on our family. She is very much encouraged by your letter and feels lightened. She is writing you separately.

I have noted the few points mentioned by you. We shall plan only Kanpur visit when Swamiji is in Delhi in April. Other places were just suggestions and may be considered for future. Kamaths told us about the change in their program. Now the cassettes may be sent with Balanji when he visits Ashrama. Swamiji may send his blessings for the book at his convenience. The publishing of it has been planned after sometime.

We are concerned about your health. It has to be taken care of. Hopefully all necessary care is being taken.

Things over here are fine. Delhi is quite cold these days. Due to exam of Amit and Rohit, we could not go for *satsang* at ashrama on 10th January. However we shall go on 24th. Sometime we face conflict in the matter as other pressures work on mind. Hopefully such conflicts will resolve with time. But one thing is sure, we are more and more at peace with ourselves and the atmosphere at home is becoming increasingly harmonious. We look at it as the result of

Guru's grace. However moments of despair come at times, particularly when the problems of children overtake us. Perhaps Aruna will touch upon this aspect in more detail.

Regarding my spiritual and devotional routine, I am trying to improve it, though for various reasons it gets disturbed. I am almost regular as far as reading is concerned. I have gone through two books of Swamiji since he left Delhi. "Words that illumine" is being gone through repeatedly. In fact the first thing in the morning is to go through few thoughts from the book. Its Hindi translation is also going on. However I have not been able to practice meditation, though I have started sitting for sometime in the evenings. I need your guidance in this regard. The office work is quite light and will continue to remain so for some more time. So I am trying to utilize it as much as I can.

I am closing here but before that a word about your handwriting. It is really very good and has fascinated us.

Please convey my *pranams* to Rev. Swamiji and Swami Nirviseshanandaji. Pranams to other inmates of the Ashrama.

Pranams to you again

Humbly yours
Rakesh

*****

7

First Visit to Ashrama

Thereafter, our correspondence was not very frequent. However, in each letter we received from the Ashrama, there were pearls of wisdom which gave us constant guidance. We planned our first visit to Narayanashrama Tapovanam, Thrissur, in March 1993 and stayed there from 27th March to 3rd April. Our elder son, Amit, could not join but the younger son, Rohit, did. The stay in the Ashrama was a unique experience for us. Kerala as a whole is a beautiful state full of nature's bounty; it was all the more so in the Ashrama and around. The stay arrangements were simple but quite comfortable. Every minute requirement of the devotees was taken care of meticulously and we learnt that this in itself was a *Sadhana*. The message was that, day to day minor activities are not divorced from spirituality and if they are done with devotion, it is equally a spiritual activity.

The morning and evening *satsang* with Swamiji and other inmates were the best part of the learning. Wisdom was imparted through informal as well as formal discussions. Interaction with inmates as well as visitors was also equally enriching. Overall, we felt very homely in that beautiful part of the country, which also indicates the greatness of our country. We left the Ashrama with a heavy heart after staying for about a week, but had been greatly enriched in the process. Again, there was exchange of a few letters after this visit.

First Visit to Ashrama

Poojya Swamiji's birthday falls on May 13. In 1993 he turned 60 and we celebrated the occasion at the place of a close devotee, Mrs. Silva Roy. At that time she lived in Safdarjung Development Area (SDA). She was from Russia (Estonia) and her husband was a chemical engineer. The devotion of Mrs. Roy was exemplary and it was always a great pleasure to be in her company.

During this period, my father was not well and he expired on May 19, 1993, in my home town, Purkazi in Muzaffarnagar District of Uttar Pradesh. My father was born in the year 1900 and was about 93 at the time of his death. I have already written about the salient features of his personality. He lived a long, simple, contented and useful life. His departure brought a new phase in our life. My mother was alive at that time and lived for a few more years. Swamiji sent a brief but very inspiring letter on this occasion. I am reproducing this letter here.

> Narayanashrama Tapovanam,
> Venginissery, P.O. Paralam, Trichur,
> Kerala, India-680575
> 9th June 1993
>
> Dear and blessed Rakesh and Aruna:
> Hari Om Tat Sat.
>
> The postcard intimating the news about your father's departure to *Vaikuntha* came here in time. The earlier letter also.
>
> I hope the last phase was peaceful. Separation from one's dear and near ones is always unpleasant; but when the elderly depart, there is greater reconciliation because of age and attendant features. To be serving the old, and being present to do whatever is necessary for them during and after departure is a rare opportunity. It fulfils and teaches in many ways.
>
> I hope all the usual ceremonial routines have been gone through well, which in a way is a great satisfaction and relief.

The better part will be to pursue wholeheartedly in one's life the cherished values and ideals of the father. That will be an endless service and contribution to the departed one. One always learns from others, and the lessons and revelations a parent offers stand unique.

Please tell your brothers, Shri Suraj Prakash and Dr. Chandra Mohan, also of my fond sharing on this occasion of the loss and absence.

May you have all the strength, composure and reconciliation to withstand the new phase.

My love, regards and co-feelings to all the younger ones also, especially Amit and Rohit, whom I know. The others in the Ashrama also send you hearty feelings on the occasion.

Love and sivasis,

Yours
Swamiji

It was now time to further expand our vision and be more universal in our thinking. The yearly *Daana Satras* of Swamiji was an inspiring event for us and, for the first time, we understood the sublimity of participation in such an event. The manner in which it is conducted is in itself a great message. Though I could myself participate in the process later, its description was always enriching.

*****

8

Swamiji Visits Kanpur

After *Guru Purnima* in 1993, we planned to organize Swamiji's talks at various institutions in Delhi under the auspices of Brahmavidya Centre. For this a request letter was sent to them indicating suggested topics. Many good institutions responded positively and Swamiji's talks were organized in many of them during his Delhi visit in October-November 1993. These included the Indian Institute of Technology (IIT), Food Corporation of India (FCI), Institute of Secretarial Training and Management (ISTM) and few others. This was a very successful initiative which proved that spiritual talks are always helpful if they are delivered in a practical manner. This also set a broader role for Swamiji in future. These talks were in addition to regular discourses which Swamiji used to conduct during his annual visits. I, in particular, was not only happy in being a part of this exercise, but was also a significant beneficiary of these talks.

    Simultaneously, I was trying to plan a visit of Swamiji to Kanpur. Swamiji was himself keen to spread his message in the Hindi belt of North India. He always wished to develop a large group to strengthen the deeper notes of the nation's culture and its personal, social and national integrity. This intention of Swamiji was very clear from his letter dated September 16, 1993, to Mr. K. K. Krishnan, an officer at Kanpur who had worked with me.

Narayanashrama Tapovanam,
Venginissery, P.O. Paralam, Trichur,
Kerala, India-680575
16th September 1993.

Dear and blessed soul, Sri Krishnan:

Hari Om Tat Sat. Your nice letter of 11th to hand. I understand your interest and intentions. So you plan to come here next time you visit Kerala. Meanwhile, Sri Mittal is planning our visit to Kanpur, and so we should be meeting there. In whichever way it will be, may your heartiness and intentions be furthered and fulfilled.

Sri Mittal, committed to an unusual note of spiritual interests and seeking, seems also to be impelled to share his mind and heart with others, so that a larger group may get formed and strengthened to the deeper notes of the Nation's culture, given to personal, social and national integrity, a deep sense of commitment and an ever-increasing spirit of socialness and community welfare. It is these traits that have made our nation so long standing in its basic cohesion and strength. And alas, which, of late have been threatening to erode unduly.

Generally unselfish thinking and social notes adorn the minds of only very few, and only a handful of persons apply this quality in a practical and committed manner. If Sri Mittal and you have an affinity or correspondence, in this regard, it is an unusual fortune of the country and people. May everything here and above favour you with its choicest strength and blessings, so that the great spirit can be furthered; and both you as individuals, and a section around you, as a group, be benefited as a result. I give you my personal appreciation, love and benedictions.

Have health, strength, prosperity and peace.

Sri K. K. Krishnan
Chief Manager, Finance,
U.P. Export Corporation Ltd.
B-27 Sarvodaya Nagar, Kanpur

Your own self.
(Swami Bhoomananda Tirtha)

This letter of Swamiji filled us with immense enthusiasm to organize his Kanpur visit in the best possible manner. His stay arrangement was made at a friend's place and we were also to stay there. The whole family took it as a great opportunity for itself and took care of all the requirements. The head of the family was Shri Bharat Bhushan Gupta, a founder member of Kabir Peace Mission and a spiritual thinker in his own right. Other members of the mission also took keen interest in Swamiji's visit. Our President, Dr. Krishna Bihari Agrawal; Secretary, Shri Pradeep Goenka and Trustee, Dr, Rajesh Agrawal, all took great pains to make the visit successful. The visit was from November 1 to November 5, 1993, and thus we spent the second anniversary of our initiation in the holy company of Swamiji, Nutan Swamiji and Ma Gurupriya, at Kanpur.

Swamiji won the hearts of Kanpur-*walas* in his first appearance. It was also his first speech in Hindi from a public platform. Though he had some hesitation about it, his Hindi was very well received by the audience. For them, it was a new experience in spirituality. Swamiji spoke mainly on Bhagavad Gita, but he connected real life situations with its message lucidly and clearly, something the audience was not used to earlier. This resulted in an instant rapport between them and the whole programme was highly successful.

Swamiji paid several home visits and granted many personal interviews during this period. The media also covered his visit very well and all this resulted in a reverential request for his regular visits in the future. Being in the company of Swamiji all through this period, I was a great beneficiary of his spiritual wisdom.

During my return journey from Kanpur to New Delhi, I spent about five hours in the company of Swamiji. It was, again, a new experience for me. Initially, I was a little unsure of my conversation with him, but very soon we established a rapport in our communication. All through this journey Swamiji treated me like a friend and I learnt a lot from him. I could also share my views on various issues which normally is not possible with a spiritual master. For the first time I realized that spirituality is not a part-time activity, it is a whole-time pursuit which must reflect in our all activities.

After reaching Thrissur, both Swamiji and Ma Gurupriya wrote us very affectionate and meaningful letters, dated November 30, 1993. Since these letters contained great messages, I am reproducing both of them here.

Swamiji's Letter

30 Nov 1993

Dear and blessed Rakesh and Aruna:

Hari Om Tat Sat. Ever since we reached here, the mind has been bringing forth various memories of the Delhi and Kanpur sojourns. With Kanpur, Aruna and you both also have a special place. The visit, though first, was arranged well. I also cherished the long chat you had with me on way back. Aruna had managed things very well. Some of the dialogues she had with Ma, told me by Ma, are very refreshing. It is very strange that in human life, the usual relationships with blood and matrimonial persons, have a binding and tensing effect; whereas the same relationship with Mahatmas has just the opposite effect. Both relationships proceed from the same mind. Yet see the difference! It was in this light that I heard some of the accounts narrated by Ma, about Aruna and the Gupta family members. May all of you be enriched and blessed by the *satsang* and its sublimity.

You have done a lot of work dedicatedly to arrange the few institutional talks. I have often thought about such appearances and the interceptions the listeners get from a spiritual person. One thing is that they would come to know that the spirituality is not all that religious alone. There is an appreciable measure of knowledge and intellectual worth in the spiritual persons, or at least can be. Their attitude, if at all, changes towards the subject and the people. And to that extent our role and what we represent gets propagated. Whether this in itself is sufficient as a goal or something more tangible should be had, is a point to be evaluated. Do this from your own level and contact. And let us see. Besides what I have thought and assessed, whether there is anything from the professional angle, is something that those like you can determine. However, if such talks are to be given again, we must be able to pool some thoughts and ideas, which will be more profession-oriented.

I feel quite concerned about Rohit not giving enough attention to his studies. He does not have so much bodily disability as the brother has. And naturally we expect him to do much better in the matter of movements and activity as also studies. Belonging to you, as parents, and having a good heredity, if it does not come up with studies, the gap and affliction will be too much. Please tell him these words dearly, and ask him to give me his response directly. The words of elders have to be listened to, till one becomes a full-fledged elder. Even elders have to listen to their friends and well wishers. One's own Intelligence will not be fool-proof or adequate.

Here are a few lines of a poem, which greatly cause a transformation in thinking:
There is no thing we cannot overcome;
Say not thy evil instinct is inherited.
Or that some trait inborn makes thy whole life forlorn,
And calls down punishment that is not merited.
Back of thy parents and grandparents lies,
The great Eternal Will! That too is thine.
Inheritance - strong, beautiful, divine
Sure lever of success for one who tries.
There is no noble height thou canst not climb;
All triumphs may be thine in Time's futurity,
If whatsoever thy fault, thou dost not faint or halt;
But lean upon the staff of God's security.
Earth has no claim the soul cannot contest;
Know thyself part of the Eternal Source;
Naught can stand before thy spirit's force;
The soul's Divine Inheritance is best.

He will do well to ponder over these lines, which have the fire of strength and inspiration in them.

Every day and week is precious for the student. He should not repent later. Instead strive hard right now. We can only speak and help. Actual effort he alone can make. And he should.

Come to an agreement that you will not get angry with him, provided he does not give any cause for you to feel bad about his not doing well in studies, and in general. Every parent is impatiently waiting for his children to grow up and become responsible. Right when responsibility is seen in the children, parents would automatically recede, and look for help and assistance from the children. So they should not mis-value the whole role and relationship.

Remember what I told you in the field of *sadhana*. Both of you should spend some time in trying to get absorbed into your own bosom, with relaxation and fondness. This is a must. Let me know how this effort fares and progresses.

It has been difficult to get to the Ashrama routines after such a long *satsang* with all of you. It is so every time. This time it has been even more so.

Dr. S. N. Prasad from Bombay has come and is with us. A very exemplary type of seeker, with 24 years of association with me.

I have written to your two brothers: Gupta (family) and Agarwal. Please tell your doctor brother and the other Doctor who attended on me while I was sick. May they have health, inward enrichment and further success in life.

Love and Sivasis,

Yours
Swamiji

Ma Gurupriya's Letter

30th November 1993

"Spiritual wisdom frees the mind and intellect of their shackles, building greater and greater behavioural skill and harmony. By eliminating conflicts it promotes the spirit of reconciliation. Ability to assimilate adversities and the readiness to make sacrifices are pronounced in a seeker. Neither is the knower confronted by the world, nor is the world confronted by him. Both are beautifully complements."

Swamiji.

Dear and blessed Rakesh and Aruna,

Hari Om Tat Sat. While I write the letter my heart gets full of love and fondness for you and the children. Ever since we have returned, I wanted to write to you, but the amount of piled-up work and a natural lethargy to get back to the usual routine, presence of visitors (one of whom was my father) gave me very little time to sit for replying letters. While carrying on with the usual domestic chores or when I am alone at my table writing for *Vicharasethu*, many a time your faces and voice become vivid in the mind. May Lord bless you always with peace, happiness and contentment. May the simplicity and heartiness that He has already blessed you with grow everyday spreading joy to more and more people.

We very often speak about our Kanpur visit. Everything was well arranged and with love and heartiness. We never felt that we were meeting the group for the first time and felt so much at home and so close! Swamiji and Naya Swamiji have already written to Kanpur; I would write shortly.

It was good that Aruna decided to make herself free and stayed with us in Kanpur. We missed Rakesh ji. Amit and Rohit had to sacrifice their comfortable life at home no doubt, but they should be appreciated for having done this sacrifice in order to allow their mother to have *Satsang*, which is a very rare fortunate opportunity in one's life. I remember how Aruna used to remain alert even in sleep thinking she should not miss if we called her; how she used to work with an attitude of loving service. Let our Lord's Grace be with her always giving her self-contentment and joy.

We were missing you both during our next few days stay in Delhi. This time the *Vishnusahasranama Yajna* was grand and we remembered you quite a lot.

After return, we are slowly settling down to our normal routine. My father came for an eight days' stay. He came from Bangalore, where my brother stays. My mother did not come. My father wished to have some instructions recorded by Swamiji for children to grow in discipline, studies, concentration, to develop faith in God and devotional routines.

The cassette has come out very well, intercepted by *sloka*-chanting by myself and Naya Swamiji and concluding with *Nama Japa* by *Chhota* Swamiji Naya Swamiji and myself.

How are all of you? How are Rohit and Amit? Has Deepak come to work? If he has, then please convey my fond love to him. Handle him fondly but tactfully so that he turns out to be a good help. At the same time, help him by imparting to him basic refinement, good manners, alertness and readiness to serve lovingly.

Please convey to Mr. And Mrs Ramani and Balaji our fond remembrance.

For all of you my love, fondness and blessings,

Ma

P.S. The *atta laddus* were liked by Swamiji. We too took it as *prasada*. The packing and wrapping were also expressing elegance and good taste.

Aruna, please send the recipe for this *laddu*.
Write in details.

The message which comes out of such responses is that a truly spiritual person is like any worldly person. The only difference is that while he or she has all the human qualities and expresses them lavishly, he or she is not affected by them. That is why Swamiji often says that while living in the world, be a great enjoyer and equally be a great sufferer.

KANPUR VISIT OF SWAMIJI (November, 1993)

Swami Nirviseshananda Tirtha, Swami Bhoomananda Tirtha and Ma Gurupriya at the residence of Shri K.B. Agarwal President Kabir Peace Mission.

Swami Bhoomanandaji, Swami Nirviseshanandaji & Ma Gurupriya with Smt. Sushma Agarwal & Shri K.B. Agarwal.

Swami Bhoomanandaji in conversation with the Trustees of Kabir Peace Mission Shri B.B. Gupta, Shri K.B. Agarwal & Shri Rakesh Mittal.

Swami Bhoomanandaji, Nutan Swamiji and Ma in the company of devotees at Kanpur.

Author in the company of H.H. Dalai Lama on the eve of New Millennium at Sarnath, Varanasi. (31.012.1999)

Author in the company of Shri Narendra Modi during 'The Millennium World Peace Summit of World Religious and Spiritual Leaders' held at UNO Headquarters. New York from 28th August to 31st August 2000

LUCKNOW VISIT OF SWAMIJI (March, 2001)

Hon. Governor of UP Shri Vishnu Kant Shastri greeting Swami Bhoomananda Tirtha.

Mayor of Lucknow Dr. S.C. Rai welcomes Swami Bhoomanand Ji.

Smt. Aruna Mittal garlanding Ma Gurupriya in the public programme.

Swamiji addressing the audience at Lucknow.

LUCKNOW VISIT OF SWAMIJI (November, 2015)

A view of 'Smriti Bhavan' at Lucknow constructed in the memory of Shri Amit Mittal and Shri Rohit Mittal.

Swami Bhoomanandaji, Ma Gurupriya with Shri Rakesh Mittal and Smt. Arun Mittal after inagurating 'Smriti Bhavan'

...vami Bhoomanandaji lights the lamp after the inaguration of 'Smriti Bhavan'. Standing with him are Dr. K.B. Agarwal and Shri Rakesh K. Mittal.

President Ram Krishna Math Swami Muktinathanandaji Lucknow accompanies Swami Bhoomanandaji in 'Lighting of Lamp' during 'Smriti Bhavan' inauguration.

Smt. Aruna Mittal in the holy company of Ma Gurupriya.

Swami Bhoomanandaji delivering talk on the subject 'Equanimity in Life' after inaugurating 'Smriti Bhavan' on 25th November, 2015.

It means one should always be above the narrowness of existence. Many of us interpret spirituality in such a wrong manner that the word itself frightens us and we don't even try to know it. A true spiritual master not only makes our inner life beautiful but also our external life. Thus, our whole existence becomes a joyful voyage instead of a painful stagnation. In other words, a spiritual person is not a stone without any feelings or emotions but even more sensitive to the environment, without being a victim of the same. This was something which created a deep impression in my life and benefited me immensely.

*****

9

Turning into an Author

After coming in contact with Swamiji I had become even more contemplative and started expressing observations in the form of small write-ups. The number of these write-ups was growing with time. I used to wonder about their quality and content. This made me feel that I was only an instrument in writing them—the inspiration was from some higher source. I distributed the copies of these write-ups among my friends and received their compliments. The idea of converting them into a book did not occur to me in the beginning. Meanwhile, I had come in contact with Mr. S. K. Ghai of Sterling Publishers Private Limited, New Delhi, through Balanji, who had been a part of publication industry for a long time.

By this time my first book under the title, *Dictionary of Positive Thoughts*, which was published at Kanpur, was getting good reviews. The presentation of the book was not very attractive and Balanji advised me approach Mr. Ghai for its publication and he readily agreed to do so. I was very happy with this development and wanted Swamiji to bless this maiden effort of mine. Swamiji accepted my request and sent his blessings soon. It conveyed a deep message to both the administration and the society. I am producing the same here for the benefit of the readers.

Blessings of Swamiji in *Dictionary of Positive Thoughts*

In the survival, growth and achievement of any society, the triple fronts, namely the HOME, the places of learning and Productivity, and the Public Administrative Machinery have always a basic and decisive role to play. The effort to instil and preserve character and quality in all these has to remain ever watchful. Neither routine dialogues nor formalized procedures and systems, nor again the regular bulk of law and revenue functions will be adequate for ensuring sustenance and growth. Only when strong values, powerful inspiration and unswerving integrity radiate from individuals and groups alike, the common mind will be rightly moulded and community performance and refinement achieved in proper measure.

A society with an ageless past, sobered and sublimated by sound reflections, can alone succeed in building the inestimable treasure of values. Much greater care and nursing is needed to enrich such a treasure generation after generation. *Subhashitas* (aphorisms and adages) of an amazing variety, updated from time to time, rendered in the nation's common language (Sanskrit), running to pages, couched in poetic rhythm and beauty, are a standing monument to the heights of excellence our people had reached in this field.

It is gratifying that a public administrator like Rakesh Mittal has loved to collect an assortment of aphorisms and string them well, making it facile to look for any particular kind at any time. His literary venture has encompassed lands beyond *Bharat* and by this he has enhanced the scope and strength of the treasure. I wish he also had recorded the source of each collection, which will go to increase its worth and amiability.

Stability of public administration consists in the devoutness with which the administrators abide by values in their task. And in this, success depends upon how well individuals and groups are able to introspect and adjudge their performance with depth and vision. None would relish to be judged by another, but equally so, no one can also eschew the heartiness to be evaluated by himself, for which knowledge, reflection and fondness of values have a paramount place.

May this collection beckon and inspire as many persons in as many fields of national life as possible.

With loving benedictions,

Swami Bhoomananda Tirtha
Narayanashrama Tapovanam
Thrissur (Kerala) 680575

This book was released in the early part of 1994 in Delhi. Many friends and devotees of Swamiji were present. Enthused with this, my writing took on a rapid pace and a good number of write-ups were collected. In a way, this was the beginning of my transformation as an author. I consider this development also a part of Swamiji's blessings.

It is also a fact that the first beneficiary of my writings was myself, and I always strove to live my life in accordance with my writings. This in itself became my spiritual *sadhana*. Swamiji visited Delhi again in March 1994 along with Nutan Swamiji and Ma Gurupriya. For the first time Swamiji organized this programme at the request of his devotees. The purpose was to have more interaction with them, and from that viewpoint, it was successful, though hectic for Swamiji. During this visit we also received a lot of guidance.

*****

10

Disharmony at Home

Despite all our efforts, disharmony used to occur in my family and we constantly addressed this issue. Swamiji gave useful tips and instructions to us which helped a lot. My letter dated April 18, 1994, to Swamiji and his reply dated May 5, 1994, are important in this respect and I am producing them below.

My Letter

O-2-1 R. K. Puram
New Delhi-110066
18th April, 1994

Rev. Swamiji, Pranam.

I rang up on 15th April and learnt from Naya Swamiji that you all have reached there comfortably. It was a long outing this time and so things will naturally take more time to settle. I hope you have recovered from the fatigue and the *Ashrama* activities are back to normal. We, the Delhi devotees, are very fortunate to have you all amidst us and to have close interaction. My family is deeply touched by your concern for all of us. Your blessings will definitely elevate us more and more and we shall prove worthy of them.

It was very nice that Aruna expressed her feelings before you and Ma and you in turn communicated to me along with your guidance. I admit that there have been occasional aberrations in our interactions but the fact is that the concern for each other has always been there. Maybe, at times it was too much and that is what has been the reason for aberrations. There is no need of going into the whole background except to say that we both came from such backgrounds where there had been no spiritual exposure. We both appreciated each other's good qualities but quite often saw conflict between our good qualities and the worldly ways. It is only after being exposed to spiritual path, that the strength of good qualities started becoming clear. The difficulty arose when I moved faster on this path and could develop conviction behind goodness. I always felt that even suffering on the path of goodness is enriching. Here was the difference with Aruna who perhaps expected goodness to be returned by goodness and felt hurt when it was not so. I do not mean to say that I never felt hurt, I also did but the difference was there. This difference at times was interpreted as lack of faith or my lack of concern towards the worldly duties. At times I desperately tried to explain and failure to do so led to aberration in the behaviour as mentioned above. I admit that there is no justification to such aberration but the point which I want to make is that there was bound to be some aberration in the absence of proper guidance and I feel that any other aberration could have been more harmful. In such a position, I do not regret them though feel very bad for them.

Another aspect is also important. My views have been different from most of my dear and near ones since childhood. Being youngest in the family, I could never express them empathically, what to say of imposing them, while I always felt strongly about them, though without knowing the reasons (perhaps it was intuitional). Thus a strong, dormant desire took root to convert those views into action and any opposition without any sound reason created reaction. This explains the problems of initial days, now it is no more.

I have written all these facts to you so that you feel assured that with your loving guidance, such aberrations will no more be there. In fact after coming in your contact, we are much more harmonious with our environment despite the tremendous pain we feel due to children.

But for your association, things would never have been different. We may not be spending much time in your company but our effort is to adopt what you say. Naturally the process takes time but we are moving ahead, there is no doubt in it. With this major aberration disappearing with your blessings, surely the progress should be faster. Now that I have taken a vow before you, your blessings become all the more necessary and I seek them from you rightfully. I have expressed myself before you fully and if I deserve, grant me your blessings. I can only assure you that I shall never misuse them.

With these words I close this letter I wanted to say all this before you but there was no occasion to do so or maybe I could not have done so. Hence this letter.

The Calcutta matter is yet to be finalized. This is keeping us in somewhat uncertain position. Yesterday Mr. K. B. Agarwal had come from Kanpur and spent few hours with us. We discussed about Amit's settlement and he has given very assuring response. Amit will go to Kanpur after his exams in June and if things work out, he may start working under his guidance. Sri Agrawal was very sorry to have missed your *Darshan* in Delhi and now looks forward to your visit to Kanpur in the month of November. The tentative dates indicated by Naya Swamiji suit very well.

Aruna and Rohit are fine. Aruna is now greatly relieved and we have had some very useful interaction in the light of your guidance. Because of Calcutta, Rohit's schooling has become little uncertain for the time being. Hopefully it will be sorted out soon.

Aruna, Amit and Rohit convey their *pranams* to you. Please convey our *pranams* to Ma and Naya Swamiji. *Pranams* to all other inmates of the Ashrama. Please write if there is any service for me.

My *pranams* to you again.

Yours humbly
Rakesh

Swamiji's Response

Narayanashrama Tapovanam
Trichur, Kerala-680575
5th May 1994

Dear and blessed Rakesh:

Hari Om Tat Sat. Your letter, touching and pleasing, arrived in time. I read it well. The intention is clear it will only strengthen your purpose. More than an explanation, it is a sharing, which always goes to lighten and ease out matters.

Life is a process of unfoldment, not achievement. I used to say this often. The initial phase of anyone's life takes place, unguided or unchosen by himself. Born of parents, bred by them, nursed by the environments, allowed the place and position each comes by somehow, this phase comes to get settled somehow. It may have good points, bad points as well.

Both will have their respective impact, true. In such a background the foreground of grown up life has to grow. The mind and temper will be pitted against this complex background. Intelligence is there to reflect, evaluate and guide.

Just like one outlives playfulness, when he becomes youthful and the old ager outlives the impatience of the youth, here too the adult person has to outlive his boyish and girlish behaviour, responses and motivations.

Thus a parent who was given to scolding and also beating (punishing) his children till they grew up to the age of 15 or 18, will and must now outlive that temper and tempest. His hands should stop rising, instead his mind and intelligence should rise and raise a new effective response and move. This has to be done. If the process gets delayed, it is wrong. Damage also will be greater.

If some are not able to outlive this way, it is failure, and is disharmonious. In fact, this is a phase of life when the grown up children impose and cause self-discipline, control and deeper levels of response in the parent.

To be a parent of kids, to be a parent of adolescents, and to be a parents of still grown up, are all different, and higher in degrees. Should not any father or mother undergo this growth and maturity? In the same way, to be able to husband a woman also calls for an emotional control and maturity. It is an opportunity, a compulsion, a new persuasion and self-discipline. Even when looked at in this way, the temperamental refinement and maturity cannot be saved, escaped.

So married life brings the instant self-control, whereby the permissible and sublimating emotional outbursts and behavioural notes are imbibed. Growth of children, likewise, instils another step in the same direction caused by the age and growth of children. All these fit in well with the graduated maturation of the adult parent. Anything discordant or uncontrollable is bad, disharmonious with the scheme of nature.

I am writing this only to reinforce your words and evaluations, and strengthen the resolve you already have with you now. In any way, you should not feel shy or hit because the subject came up for discussion. Also have no fears about 'what evaluation will now follow for me'; in the association with the Guru or *Mahapurusha*, no such feeling should be entertained. We are only to help and strengthen others, not to hinder or devalue them.

Between friends, any excess or failure is excusable. Between a couple this is all the more so. The bond of the heart is far stronger than the ties of intelligence. Aruna thus will always be wishing and striving for your welfare and Rakesh will be most concerned with her peace and well being. Any misnote is to be condoned and forgotten. And goodness and nicety alone to be remembered and enhanced.

We are getting settled to the routines here. Naya Swamiji is in touch with Lalita Didi in the matter of printing 'Vedantic Way of Living'. He has sent the back page writing selecting a picture for the purpose.

We had corrected and written the Sanskrit verses and transliteration at Delhi itself. The production with all this must be good and foolproof.

You may if necessary keep in touch with Sri Ghai. We wonder whether the book will not be published soon. Our next efforts for such printing and publishing will depend upon this instance.

I have noted about the Calcutta prospects as they stand now. May the right turn of events take place.

With love and Sivasis.

Yours Swamiji

*****

11

Transfer to Kolkata and First Guru Poornima Retreat

During the same period I got my promotion as Joint Secretary and my next posting was due. One option available to me was to go to Kolkata (then Calcutta) as Development Commissioner of Iron and Steel and the other was to wait for any other vacancy in Delhi itself. I was not able to make up my mind very clearly, but on advice from Swamiji I left the turn of events to destiny. There were pluses and minuses in both the options and nature would be the best judge.

Eventually, I was posted at Kolkata in place of my own boss. It was a field posting with a good residence and with plenty of opportunities to travel. Also, there were other facilities available at various places, like Mumbai, Chennai, and Delhi, etc. I could travel to any place in the country as and when required. All these factors made me feel happy.

My elder son Amit had cleared most of his papers in B. Com from the Indira Gandhi Open University (IGNOU). Shri K. B. Agarwal advised me to leave him in Kanpur for training in his office while completing his remaining papers and the family of Shri B. B. Gupta offered him a place in their home. With all these arrangements made, we shifted to Kolkata in the first week of July, 1994. Rohit was admitted in Kendriya Vidyalaya while Amit shifted to Kanpur.

The Kolkata stay provided us with a very good opportunity for *sadhana* and contemplation. My job required frequent touring, which I utilized in reading and writing. On the other hand, Aruna enjoyed her solitude at home and devoted a lot of time to her spiritual *sadhana*. We had some good friends at Kolkata and our hometown being quite far, there were no surprise guests!

First Guru Poornima Retreat

It was in July itself that I planned my visit to Narayanashrama Tapovanam, Thrissur, on the occasion of *Guru Poornima*. I went alone and it was my first visit on such an auspicious occasion. That year *Guru Poornima* fell on July 22. On my return to Kolkata, I wrote a note on my three day stay in the Ashrama and I am producing it below, along with my covering letter.

Rakesh K. Mittal, IAS   1-C Neelanjan
18/2 Gariahat Road, Calcutta
25th July, 1994

Rev. Swamiji, Pranams,

I reached here last night at about 1 o' clock. The flight from Madras was delayed by about two hours. Anyway, there was no problem of any kind .

I am very happy to be able to visit the Ashrama on the auspicious occasion of Guru Poornima. This was possible due to your blessings only. I am greatly touched by with the serenity of the occasion and also with the affection and love showered by all. More than anything else, was the pleasure of meeting fellow devotees. Hopefully such visits will be more frequent in future.

Aruna is very happy to receive the letter from Ma and the *prasadam*. She will be writing separately to Ma. This morning I talked to Dr. K. C. Majumdar. I am arranging to send the letter and the *prasadam* today itself. We shall ourselves visit them after sometime. I am again leaving for

Delhi on 28th July and will be back on 4th August. Thereafter, I propose to stay at Calcutta for a longer stretch.

Guru Poornima celebration shall be over by the time this letter will reach you. Please convey our pranams to Naya Swamiji, Ma, Swami Nirupamananda ji and other inmates. I shall write you later in detail.

Pranams to you again.

Yours humbly
Rakesh

Guru Poornima — A Spiritual Retreat

This year Guru Poornima fell on 22nd July. I had wished to be with Swamiji on this day at least alone if not with family. However, I was not sure about it particularly in view of my transfer to Calcutta from New Delhi. I took charge of the new assignment in the afternoon of 30th June at Delhi itself and planned to move to Calcutta with family on 9th July. The interim period was utilised for packing, loading, visiting friends and relatives and also acquainting myself with the new job of which a substantial role had to be played from Delhi. However, with the grace of God everything went on well and we reached Calcutta as per our plan. The household luggage also reached in time and we settled in our new home within two days.

I had planned my visit to the ashrama at Delhi itself and arranged tickets etc. accordingly. Though I was not able to spare more than three days in view of the initial demands of the job, I was keenly looking forward to these three days. Perhaps it was the test of my keenness that few hurdles came in the way of this programme. In the evening of 12th July, I went down with viral fever. I had an important meeting in Bombay and was scheduled to go there on the 14th. The doctor advised me to cancel the visit but I decided to postpone the visit by just a day. Again, the grace worked and I recovered sufficiently to enable me to travel within two days. The meeting went off well and I returned Calcutta on the night of 17th July. I was to leave for Madras by air on way to Thrissur on 20th July and then catch the train for Trichur in the evening. The gap between arrival of the plane at Madras and departure of the train was only a few hours. I was also to attend certain official work during this period. The plane left Calcutta on time, but soon after takeoff the captain declared some engineering problem in the plane and it landed back at Calcutta. The programme became uncertain once again because there was no guarantee of the next plane being made available immediately. Fortunately Indian Airlines, contrary to expectation, could arrange another plane within two hours and I reached Madras with sufficient margin so as to be able to attend to some of the official work and also to catch the train for Trichur. Thus the uncertainty ended and soon I was on my way to my first visit to the Ashrama on the occasion of Guru Poornima. I consider it all to be the Grace of Guru that a sincere wish of a devotee was about to be fulfilled.

The train arrived at Trichur on time, which was early morning of 21st July. An officer of the Kerala government received me at the station and arranged my halt at the Circuit House for a few hours. After taking bath, etc., I planned to visit the famous *Guruvayoor* Temple before going to the Ashrama. I informed Swamiji about this program. The officer of the Kerala govt. also accompanied me to *Guruvayoor*. In fact, he was a devotee of this temple and was very happy to learn about this program, which had not been communicated in advance. Since the time available was short and I was keen to reach the Ashrama as early as possible, he arranged a quick *Darshan*. This also happened effortlessly without any show of official authority. After the *Darshan* I reached the ashrama at about 12:30 in the afternoon, where Swamiji and other inmates were waiting for me. I prostrated before Swamiji and exchanged greetings with others. The lunch was ready, and, as is the practice in the Ashrama, the officer accompanying me and the driver were also invited for lunch, which we all took together.

A room in the new guest house was arranged for me along with Mr. A. Ramaswamy from Muscat. He too was on his first Guru Poornima retreat. Mr. Itendra Tewari was looking after the arrangements in the guest house. I was impressed by his keenness and promptness. Since I had not carried bedding, he immediately arranged one for me. After lunch, I was advised to take some rest before we met for tea in the afternoon and for briefing session about the next day's programme. The day's programme was neatly displayed at various important locations including the corridors of the guest house. During the brief period of rest, my partner, Mr. Ramaswamy, and I got acquainted with each other and we immediately developed a mutual liking. He was a young engineer settled in Muscat who, despite his young age, had very rich experiences of life to relate. It was a pleasure to meet him and interact with him.

In the afternoon, we assembled for tea, which was served with usual fondness and care. In the Ashrama, great care is extended to individual needs and I was no exception to it. I only got more than my share on account of my dietary restrictions. For me it was very touching, particularly when I find that even close relations and friends who have known me for a long time are not always able to remember these restrictions. The only problem is that I lose the freedom of violating these restrictions, which becomes possible on account of the above-mentioned forgetfulness! After tea, the detailed programme of the retreat was explained by Balanji, with the assistance of others.

I am not going into the details of the programme because it is being covered by Silvaji, but I shall touch upon the other aspects of the occasion. As far as the Guru Poornima celebration was concerned, I would only say that it was a very sublime and touching occasion. Every detail was meticulously planned. The message of Swamiji was very deep and conveyed the true relevance of the occasion. He explained that the occasion was not for the glorification of an individual saint but for honouring the tradition of *Guru-*

Shishya relationship, which is the backbone of our cultural heritage. Guru is only symbolic in the whole process as he acts as a conveyer of the message of our *Shastras* and helps his *Shishya* to achieve self-realization.

The second aspect of the retreat, which I liked more, was meeting with the fellow devotees. For me, this was more important than even to meet Swamiji. In fact, it was precisely the reason I wanted to be in the Ashrama during Guru Poornima. The rapport with all the devotees was developed instantly and one could share one's thoughts without any hesitation. I was told that the presence of devotees this year was more than usual, so much so there was some overstretching of resources. I also had an experience of the same when on the morning of 22nd July Mr. V. K. Gopalan knocked on the door of our room along with Mrs. Gopalan and a young colleague Mr. V. Shankar. Of course he did it in an appropriate manner, and the gesture was reciprocated in the same way. The result was that with them too, rapport was developed within minutes and we had very meaningful interaction during the next two days. In particular, it was a pleasure to meet Mr. Shankar, who had come for the first time at the instance of Mr. Gopalan. He had had some personal tragedy in the recent past and it was very satisfying to note that he had come to the right place in order to come to terms with it gracefully. With him, I too had some close interaction. Then there were devotees from Jamshedpur and other places. It is difficult to write about all here, but every one of them has a special place in my mind.

I will make a mention of Mrs. Venkatachalam, who happens to be the mother of a lady colleague of mine in my ministry. She had already told her mother about my visit to the Ashrama and I too had the information about her. Somehow, without having met earlier, we could immediately spot each other and thereafter she took motherly care of me. So much so, early on the morning of 23rd July, she prepared tea for me before time so that I was not inconvenienced on account of my habit of taking bed tea. I would also like to make a mention of the presence of the parents of Naya Swamiji. They attracted my instant reverence and I was deeply touched by their mental elevation because for an ordinary person, this kind of situation would not even be imaginable.

The next impressive aspect of the retreat was its true national character. There were devotees with different backgrounds from almost all parts of the country. Rarely one comes across such a diverse group with unified thinking. In a way, it was a national integration camp too.

Added to this was the spirit of service in almost all. I was of course a poor devotee in this regard who did nothing except appreciate others performing different services. I can only take the credit of my appreciation being genuine. The service which impressed me most was the delivery of hot water by Mr. Ramamurthy and Mr. Ramachandran early in the morning. Normally one could not even imagine the availability of such a service in an Ashrama but it only shows how down to earth are the concepts of our Swamiji. Incidentally, I was also a beneficiary of this service.

And lastly the loving care of Swamiji, Ma, Naya Swamiji, *Chhota* Swamiji and all other inmates of the *Ashrama* is something which leaves mark on everyone. I was to leave on the afternoon of 23rd July and without my giving even a hint, the packed food was ready along with the *prasadam* packet and a letter to my wife Aruna written by Ma. How could she find time during such a hectic period, is a mystery. Ma also gave a letter and *prasadam* for her parents in Calcutta and it was a great pleasure for me to carry the same.

I have missed many of my impressions in order to make the write up of a reasonable size. I would only say that three days spent in the Ashrama during Guru Poornima is a memorable spiritual retreat for me. I wish to attend more such occasions along with Aruna. I am sure the opportunities will come.

Rakesh K. Mittal

This visit added a new chapter in my spiritual journey.

Swamiji used to reply to each letter of mine; it may have sometimes got delayed on account of his other engagements. Each reply gave me some deeper insight into issues raised in the letter. From his letter, dated 10th August, 1994, I quote the following paragraphs:

"Have deeper and unshakeable disposition and harmonious relationship. Let there be no further slips or falls. Each should strengthen the other. Listen to and take in more. Be considerate."

"Each day must bring greater strength. For that take things with lighter note. Heaviness should be treated as a minus point for oneself. Your strength and skill lie in making every situation light. Rarely should there be any need for explosions or break down."

"Spend some time in introspection and absorption everyday even if the least possible or as much as the system needs. In that find the relief and strength as well as support you need."

These words of Swamiji became constant guidelines for me and a measure of my spiritual progress. In fact these hold good for everyone as the ultimate aim of spirituality is harmony both outside as well as within. One can oneself know the progress by honestly evaluating his or her harmony, and any cheating will not help. The effect of these words was magical and harmony kept on increasing in our lives too.

Swamiji visited Kanpur in 1994 and again in 1995, sparing few days from his Delhi annual *Gyan Satra*. Aruna and I also reached there from Kolkata, and Amit was already there. The program was again conducted successfully and Swamiji was very happy. Once again we got the opportunity of remaining in the close company of Swamiji and Ma Gurupriya. These used to be our best moments in terms of gaining spiritual wisdom. Thus these three years consecutively left a great mark upon the Hindi belt of U.P. Thereafter, he could not visit the area because of his increasingly tight programs in Delhi, and could visit it only in 2001 when he came to Lucknow.

*****

12

Inspiration for Second Book

My time in Kolkata was passing well. My official work was being appreciated by all concerned while spiritual pursuit was also going equally well. My writings were becoming more focused with a pronounced spiritual tone in them. The number of write-ups had gone up to about 50 when I decided to compile them into a book.

The write-ups were appreciated by all those who went through them. One such person was Shri Rajeshwar Prasad, IAS, who was our Director at the Mussourie Academy. He belonged to the first batch of IAS and was a man of great principles. He was very fond of religious tourism and in that connection had come to Kolkata, with his daughter, to visit Ganga Sagar. On my request they stayed with us and we visited Ganga Sagar together. This visit was in itself a great experience.

During his stay with us, Shri Rajeshwar Prasad went through my write-ups and appreciated them immensely. When I asked him about the advisability of bringing them in the form of a book, he not only recommended this strongly, but also agreed to write its foreword. Encouraged by this, I approached the publisher who agreed to publish my next book under the title, *Positive lessons from life*. Shri Rajeshwar Prasad wrote a beautiful foreword for this book and Swamiji gave his blessings, which I am reproducing here.

Blessings of Swamiji in *Positive Lessons from Life*

Undoubtedly it is knowledge or education that distinguishes man from the rest of earth's creation. And it is the actual process of learning which each person undergoes that determines his knowledge. For providing education, we have set up schools, colleges, universities, research and training centres and the like. Nonetheless, real learning always remains a process which everyone has to take up and pursue individually.

Does it, therefore, mean that learning necessarily depends upon some specific set of circumstances like place, facility and the various means and procedures evolved for the purpose? Or is there always hope for everyone to learn, no matter where he is and whatever are the factors surrounding him? This is where practical and timely lessons from actual life become paramount.

Are people, including the scholarly and the educated, given to making use of their day to day life in the world in order to become more resourceful and contented, marching towards a state of stability and fulfilment? Perhaps the answer is invariably 'no.'

It is in this context that Rakesh K. Mittal's presentation of *Positive lessons from Life* becomes helpful, illustrative and even compulsive. No matter what level or station of life one belongs to, there is a still every scope for him to learn and get enriched every day. Whether one's income is sufficient, facilities adequate, opposition stiff or risks and dangers immense, life holds ample scope to refine and moderate oneself at the sensory, mental and intellectual levels—and what more, at the core spiritual level also, where alone the human has a full prospect of becoming happy, stable and fulfilled.

To think is the supreme quality of human life. But in thinking, the thinker must always have a clear objective of getting enriched and strengthened every time. Ensuring that this is so, is the essence of positive thinking. Our mind is gifted

Inspiration for Second Book

by nature with the great ability to look at every situation and person, interpret things and events, respond and react to any episode or interaction in a beneficial, elevating manner.

In Treta Yuga in the palace of Ayodhya, *Vashishtha* gave an eighteen day tuition to Sri Rama on how to handle the mind and intelligence, making them unassailable in every way. One message in the dialogue stands out, sparkling even today as a great pointer to everyone:

> *Soonyam aakeernataam eti, Mrityurapiutsavaayate;*
> *Aapad- sampadivaabhaati, Vidvajjana- samaa game.*

Meaning: Be it a state of void, an occasion of death of a dear or near one, a situation of danger or calamity, if it is viewed and assimilated with enlightenment, in the presence of enlightened people, guided by them, it gets transformed into an inner festivity.

All the inequalities, imbalances and divergences are no doubt there in the world and people often complain about virtually everything around. But despite all these flagrant inequalities, the mind which is the real enjoyer or sufferer at every turn, is gifted with the unobliterable capacity to sublimate every outcome and interaction, so as to gain expansion and elevation every time.

Yes, such a positive note in thinking and attitude can be taken up, developed and preserved. I think Rakesh is striving to make this possible, and in the process inspiring and inducing his readers and friends to take to the same elevating path of life.

To have a Public Administrator in our midst, live and reflect such positive notes of thinking and learning, and what more, to find him articulate in doing so, is greatly fulfilling. For any administrator, to be truly representing the country's heritage and ideals, this should be an inevitable quality and virtue.

It is equally encouraging to find that another public administrator, retired from his service, puts his stamp of approval and confirmation to what Rakesh (his erstwhile student) has done. Every good teacher imparts his learning to the student only to enrich and empower him as much as possible. And if this role is rightly fulfilled, the student will become equally or more resourceful so as to impart the learning to others too. Only then the teacher's efforts bring fruition fully. The test of any good teaching is its ability to make the student a better teacher.

Well, such is the peerless tradition and culture of our land. And I am happy to note that this finds an encouraging illustration in the case of Rajeshwar Prasad and Rakesh Mittal.

I wish them all enrichment, elevation and fulfilment in their life.

Swami Bhoomananda Tirtha
Narayanashrama Tapovanam
Thrissur Kerala
28 August 1995

This book was eventually released in May 1996 at Bhartiya Vidya Bhavan in New Delhi and the function was attended by a large number of friends. Of course, it was a new experience from which I learnt that there was always a scope for improvement in any venture in life, more so in the case of a book. The editor of the book made so many corrections in its script that at one point I thought of dropping the idea of its publication but soon realized that the corrections made the text much better. This was a lesson for my ego also and thereafter I became more careful and humble in my writings.

This book was appreciated by all and I received a number of compliments for it. This encouraged me to continue writing and my write-ups became even more contemplative. This was certainly due to the influence of Swamiji in my life. In the process, my personality was getting reinforced and greater equanimity was the outcome.

*****

13

More Developments at Home

Meanwhile, efforts for the treatment of my sons were on. In April 1995, we made one more effort in India and took them to the best hospitals of Chennai and Mumbai, namely Apollo and Jaslok, respectively. At both places the diagnosis was the same and no hope was given by them except better care for prolonging life. One doctor friend at Kanpur then advised us to visit King's Hospital in London, where a doctor had worked in that field with some positive results. The same was arranged in October 1995 and the Government allowed me to visit UK on an official trip. I took my elder son Amit with me and visited the hospital. Incidentally, in the meanwhile, the concerned doctor had passed away but the hospital gave the same advice of prolonging life by better care and exercises, etc. In this trip, I also visited the Edwards Herry Spiritual Healing Centre in UK and remained in touch with it for quite some time.

This was almost the end of our efforts in the medical field. Now it was a question of accepting the reality in full measure and with grace. This was where Swamiji's blessings and guidance helped us a lot. We started looking at the situation as a larger plan of nature and stopped questioning the fairness of God. It would be wrong to say that it happened in a day but the progress towards this thinking became faster. After my UK visit and Swamiji's visit to Kanpur, we brought Amit with us to Kolkata, leaving future happenings in the hands of God. This was not a helpless surrender but a positive faith that events would take their own course in the best possible manner.

We were in Kolkata for full two years. Swamiji visited our home during this time while on his way to Jamshedpur. Once I also went to Jamshedpur and met Nutan Swamiji's parents. It was during the time when Swamiji was not there. It was a great pleasure to meet Nutan Swamiji's father, who was very proud of his *sanyasi* son. At that point I realized that *sanyasa* is a much higher state of mind and not all were capable of reaching that state. I also realized that a *sanyasi* need not be a person with strange habits and looks. He or she moved around in the world like a normal person but remained detached from it. This is what all the scriptures in general and Gita in particular advise us to do. Once such a state of mind is achieved, all the seeming conflicts between the secular and the spiritual melt away and one can float in the world with joy. Swamiji's association was gradually taking us to that state.

My deputation in the GOI was to end in July 1996, and I wanted to get posted to Lucknow and also to live in our own house there. Accordingly, I requested the UP Government, stating the problem of my sons, and indicated the same to my tenant in Lucknow. Both promised to cooperate.

It was now a question of engaging Amit. He was soon going to complete his graduation and it was not possible to keep him away from us. I was, therefore, thinking of some private venture for him, but I was not confident of the efficacy of this. Here also Divine Grace unexpectedly manifested. In May 1996, when I went to Gujarat as an election observer, on my way I stayed at Mumbai for a night. There I consulted an elderly friend of mine who was the Chairman of IDBI at that time. Without my asking, he offered a job for Amit in SIDBI, which was a subsidiary of IDBI at that time, with its headquarters at Lucknow. It was something beyond my expectations and I took it as a blessing of Swamiji. Thereafter my worry about Amit had almost disappeared as far as his engagement was concerned.

We came to Lucknow in the mid of July where I was posted as MD of UP Agro Corporation. Soon after Amit's graduation result was out in September 1996, he was appointed in SIDBI Head Office at Lucknow, where he continued to work till he passed away in May 2013.

At Lucknow, I came in contact with *Prajapita Brahmakumaris Ishwariya Vishwa Vidyalaya*, which had its centre near my residence. I had known this organization from my time in Kanpur itself, but at Lucknow I came in its close contact. The centre in-charge, Radha Behn, also invited me to attend an administrative officers' conference at Mount Abu in October 1996 as a speaker. It was my first visit to the headquarters of this organization and I was quite impressed by its working and the sincerity of those who worked for the organization. Since then I have been in close touch with this organization and have attended several of its programmes from time to time at various places.

In 2002 we took our sons to this organization's Global Hospital at Mount Abu for Magnetic Therapy treatment, which gave them some temporary relief. However, it did not continue for long. Swamiji also visited their new centre when he came to Lucknow later. Thus, the Brahmakumaris organization also played an important role in my spiritual journey and influenced me by its spread all over the world as well as by its smooth working.

*****

14

Establishment of CIRD in Delhi

In October 1997, I was posted as Housing Commissioner of UP. We had projects all over the State, including Ghaziabad, adjacent to Delhi. At that time Swamiji was looking for an appropriate piece of land around Delhi for his Ashrama. In March 1998, when Swamiji was in Delhi for his *Gyan Satra*, I visited him along with the Chairman of the Housing Board, Shri Mahesh Dutt Sharma. During the meeting, we learnt about the search for land by Swamiji. My Chairman immediately offered him land in Vasundhara scheme of Ghaziabad. He also wondered why I had not thought of it earlier. On a formal application made by Narayanashrama Tapovanam, the Board decided to allot two acres of land in its Vasundhara scheme at Ghaziabad on educational institution rates.

The decision of the Board was published adversely in newspapers, at the instance of some vested interests. Even my name was dragged in on account of my association with Swamiji. I knew the dirty politics of the organization and that was why I had not taken personal interest in land allotment to Swamiji. It was only my Chairman who had insisted on allotment and took a firm stand despite all the adverse publicity. My strength was that I was neutral in the matter and believed that the decision was for a good cause. Eventually things became clear to critics also and the matter was settled amicably. This was also a divine decision and today the residents of Vasundhara feel grateful for the Ashrama, which is known as the Centre for Inner Resource Development (CIRD). This also strengthened my belief that right decisions taken with a detached mind are protected by divine forces.

Swamiji completed all the formalities stipulated in the allotment letter within time and very soon construction work also started. The first phase of the construction was completed in the year 2000 and the CIRD started functioning in the same year. In the meantime I got transferred to another post in May 1999.

CIRD is now the base for Swamiji's activities in and around Delhi. It functions in the spirit of an *ashrama:* **'An abode of learning and growing with value orientation in the close company of the Teacher.'** The human mind has an unlimited potential to expand and grow in any dimension. It can assimilate and harmonize any external situation. CIRD is meant to guide individuals in knowing and utilizing this power by a subtle process of personality development through wisdom orientation.

With the establishment of CIRD near Delhi, it became easier for the devotees of North India to remain in close touch with Swamiji, Nutan Swamiji and Ma Gurupriya. They started coming here twice a year. I was a special beneficiary of this development as in all my visits to Delhi I used to stay in the Housing Board guest house at Vasundhara. When CIRD came into existence, I was again posted as Housing Commissioner for about a year and even the minor hurdles related to the Ashrama were sorted out. Thereafter, my CIRD visits became regular and my spiritual growth continued under the loving guidance of Swamiji.

*****

15

More Writings and Books

In August 2000, the United Nations had organized a meet of world religious and spiritual leaders at UN Headquarters, New York. This was called "The Millennium World Peace Summit". Swamiji was also invited to attend this summit along with two disciples. I had come to know about this program in October 1999 and entertained a wish to attend it. As Swamiji was not in a position to go, I requested Swamiji to recommend me and my wife for participation. Swamiji was kind enough to do so and our names were accepted by the organizers. I prepared a paper for this summit under the title "Spirituality and the World Peace" and expressed all my spiritual wisdom gathered by that time while writing the paper. In times to come, this paper of mine became very popular and useful, and I bow down before the grace showered on me by Swamiji. I am producing this paper here.

Spirituality and the World Peace

It is very heartening that the UNO has called the spiritual leaders of the world to discuss peace right at the beginning of the twenty-first century, which also happens to be the beginning of a new millennium. It shows that the United Nations appreciate how important and holy are the places of spiritual leaders in the society and what their thoughts and actions can, in reality, mean in bestowing a better order of things for the human society and improving the environment.

The twentieth century has seen mind-boggling growth in the field of science and technology leading to tremendous economic growth. The industrial revolution in a greater part of the world has changed the face of the earth and its people beyond recognition. With all the means of communication at our command, today, the world has become a global village. All this should have led to a happier, prosperous, peaceful and harmonious society. Unfortunately, it has not been so. On the contrary, the society and the individuals, in general, are much less happy in comparison to their forefathers. This situation has developed in all fields, namely social, political, economic and even religious. Obviously this is a matter of great concern and in this background the meet of world spiritual leaders assumes a great importance.

At this occasion, it is worthwhile to recall the **'World Parliament of Religions'** at Chicago held in the year 1893. Swami Vivekananda of India at that time emphasized the need of the science coming closer to the religion in order to eradicate physical poverty. According to him the poverty is the greatest curse to mankind and unless it is taken care of, religion has no meaning. Today what seems to have happened is just the opposite. Those who have been able to remove physical poverty are facing a different kind of poverty which has taken away the pleasure of physical prosperity also. Therefore, this meet has altogether a different agenda before itself. In brief, the agenda is to arrive at an optimum mix of the two kinds of prosperities so that human life becomes happy and harmonious in true sense. It has to be established and understood by all that science and religion are complementary to each other and their co-existence is a must. While science leads to the outer development, it is religion which takes care of the inner development. Unless both are taken care of, the development of human personality will always be lop-sided and peace will remain an illusion.

This is possible only when **'Religion'** and **'Science'** both are understood in correct perspective. If this can be done, the seeming conflict between the two will disappear on its own. The success of this meet, therefore, will mainly depend upon the achievement of this objective. The information technology available today, has also to play a very important role in the achievement of this objective. Fortunately, the leaders in the field of 'Information Technology' have also realized this need as is evident from the role CNN is going to play in the success of this meet.

Let us first try to understand what is meant by religion. If the role of religion is considered rightly, all problems relating to it will be solved. The scriptures say that religion is something to guide one's conduct in life so as to manifest the divinity within. As a constitution is required for running an organization or the government, in the same way religion is necessary to live life harmoniously. Thus religion may be called the **'constitution of life'** and is an internal need of man. The principles laid down in any scripture are not the dictates of an individual person; they embody the experiences of elevated souls. Some of principles were relevant in the periods when they were enunciated and now need amendment. It is like amendments in the constitution of a country from time to time as circumstances change while the preamble remains the same. Similarly, while different practices are advocated in different religions from time to time, the basics remain the same. The variation in practices is not due to anything being wrong with them, they only indicate the evolution of life. Human life is subject to change and, therefore, some practices of life also change. If such changes are not made, people abandon religion and the very purpose of having a religion is lost. Even the basic principles of religion have been reinterpreted from time to time and place to place. This led to the birth of different religions. If we look upon various religions from this viewpoint, we will develop reverence for all of them and the religion will become a great binding force in the world.

Unfortunately, it has not happened and today the religion is a misunderstood and misinterpreted word. It needs examination as to why it so happened. This examination is required from scientific, economic, political and social viewpoint. A feeling prevails that the religion is in conflict with the progress in all these areas. Unless this feeling is removed, the religion will fail to play its intended role.

We all are aware of the revolution that has come about all over the world in the field of science. It is believed that the scientific progress in the past fifty years has been greater than in the previous 2000 years. This has affected human life. The change was so fast that man was not ready for it. **'Darwin's Theory of Evolution'** tells us that internal change (physical and intellectual) in human beings takes place gradually in accordance with the environment. If the external change is very fast, there occurs a gap between it and the internal change. This is what has happened in present times. Internal change has not been able to keep pace with the change in the external environment. In other words, we may also say that religion has not been able to keep pace with the change in the field of science and allied areas. This led to the feeling that religion was no more relevant. The problem started from here.

For some time people did not realize the consequences because the glamour of scientific progress diverted their attention from the fundamental principles of life. They felt that science had answers to all their problems of life. But when they realized the limitations of science and turned towards religion, it had gone into the hands of those people who could not interpret religion in a scientific manner, and people were not prepared to accept the traditional approach. This gave rise to conflict between science and religion. People, in general, took it as a limitation of religion.

The economic revolution all over the world has also affected religion. Religion emphasizes the need to reduce one's desires and practise sacrifice. But economic progress implies multiplication of needs. Today the scale of progress of a nation is judged by its consumption level. Economic development is also viewed by parameters like **'Gross National Income'** or **'Per Capita Income'** and not in terms of **'Gross National Happiness'**. All this gives the impression that there is a conflict between economic development and religion, because if the principles of religion are adopted, there would be no room for economic development. In reality, it is not so and there is need to remove this impression. Preachers of religion did not do this, which created a wrong impression about religion.

Changes in the field of politics have also affected religion greatly. As long as there was no degradation of political values, religion was not misused. But with selfishness and parochialism on the rise, religion has been grossly misused in many parts of the world. This has also created a narrow approach to religion. Similarly, changes in social values have affected religion adversely. In today's society, achievement of success means everything. Be it in the field of education, trade, science or industry, means have become secondary to goals. Whatever means lead to goal quickly are considered acceptable. Even harming others is not considered bad if it is found helpful. In this rat race, people think of only self-interest. But religion tells us to think only of the welfare of others. So much so, even harming oneself for the sake of others is advocated. Thus, there appears to be a conflict between the prevailing norms of the society and the principles of religion.

Thus, today man takes a very narrow view of religion and instead of considering it something essential, he believes that it is a hurdle in his growth. Therefore, there is need to define and propagate religion properly. In present times, religion will have to be defined scientifically to show that it is an essential need in the scientific, economic, social, and even in political fields. Many have worked and many more are working in this direction, but their message has not spread sufficiently. Today people raise questions, to which religion must provide suitable answers and the guardians of religion have to do so. Otherwise, a false view of religion will continue in the minds of the people and it will fail in achieving its objective.

It has to be clarified that science has never had any conflict with religion. Even in ancient times, scientific progress had reached great heights and using scientific facilities was never considered anti-religion. In fact, proper use of such facilities helps in leading a religious life. Today we are able to do many things much more conveniently which was not possible in earlier times. Religion is, however, against misuse of scientific knowledge and its achievements because this is harmful to mankind. That is to say, it is essential to have control over oneself so that one does not become a slave or victim of the products of science. In that case science becomes a cause of misery instead of being a boon. When proper coordination is kept between science and religion, life becomes more pleasuresome at the individual and the social level.

Similarly, there is no conflict between economic development and religion. Every religion advocates that the basic needs of man should be met first, because the mind cannot be healthy unless the body is healthy. Therefore, taking proper care of the body is a religious act. However today, economic development is considered to be consuming more resources than needed. This is improper at the individual as well as the social level. The mind of a man, who consumes or acquires more than what is required, can never be at peace. It affects both him, and the society, adversely. The earth has enough resources to meet the needs of all, but not the greed of even few. Therefore, the distribution of resources should be as uniform as it is in a family, for the whole world is itself a family. When all members of the society get an opportunity to lead a life which enables them to meet their essential needs, economic development will be very fast. Today, the majority of the people in the world are poor. This has affected economic development adversely and given rise to tension due to income disparities. Religion advocates reduction of desires because the earth's resources can meet only the essential needs. Though some of us may use these resources beyond our needs for a limited period, but by doing so we are only creating problem for others as well as for the future generations. Excessive exploitation of natural resources is in this sense against religious conduct and we are already paying a heavy price of it in the form of environmental pollution as well as natural calamities. Thus, it becomes clear that correct interpretation of religion will not only lead to greater economic development but that will be in tune with the nature leading to peaceful co-existence of all.

In the field of politics also, use of religion has become an important issue. In ancient times, particularly in India, Kings used to honour spiritual masters and also acted upon their advice. In the famous epic of Mahabharata, it has been said that a king should not consider himself to be a ruler but should be one ruled by righteousness. It shows that religion has always had a role in politics. Mahatma Gandhi believed that it is not possible to separate religion from politics. But what kind of religion are we talking about? A religion which has been distorted should have no place in politics. Selfish people who interfere in politics in the name of religion also should have no role to play in this field. Religion can have a place in politics only when these two factors are not there. Mahatma Gandhi used to talk about the synthesis between religion and politics in this light. Whenever there has been ethical coordination between religion and politics, society has remained harmonious and peaceful.

Religion has a bearing also in the area of social evils, prevailing in the various parts of the world. While many practices, which have now assumed vulgar shapes, started with the sanction of the religion, it failed to make necessary amends in them with changing time. As a result an impression exists that religion either supports them or is helpless in checking them. The truth of the matter is that no religion supports these social evils and there is no place for them in religious conduct. The same can be said about the rituals of various religions. They all have a scientific basis, though not explained to people or amended with time as per the changing need. For this reason also, there has been difficulty in understanding religion.

Today, there is need to place religion in its right perspective and I suppose this is the main objective of this meet. This work cannot be left to the preachers only, though they have a very important role to play. For this, every responsible section of the society will have to come forward. Religion is not something which can be understood only by reading books, attending discourses or following certain rituals. Religion is something which has to be lived every moment of life. On the surface, different religions may look different but their fundamental principles are the same and they tell us the correct way to lead a meaningful and peaceful life. Wherever a society has followed religion in its right form, there has been prosperity and happiness in true sense.

When religion is understood and adopted with this background, it becomes **'Spirituality'**. Even science has now established that the whole cosmos is interconnected and interdependent. Religion has been saying so in a different form. When we talk of a **'Super Power'** or **'God'**, it only implies that there is something common in all the creation of nature. The name given to this common entity may be different but the essence and the intention is the same. When we see the world around us with this common factor in mind, love and compassion becomes a very natural phenomenon. It is not difficult to establish or appreciate that even for mundane existence, interdependence is a must and we cannot think of any life in isolation. In the field of commerce and industry, the interdependence is all the more necessary. Creation of organization like WTO is a pointer in this direction only. It is now being growingly realized that poverty in some part of the world is not only a curse to that part but also a threat to those who are rich. Efforts of the developed nations to create markets or tap them in developing nations only indicates that even prosperity cannot survive in isolation. Unless all grow together, isolated growth becomes a menace after a period and creates disharmony and tension.

The world is passing through such a phase today and is desperate to find answer to the problem of peace. **'Prosperity'** and **'Peace'** today appear to be opposed to each other. The external sciences have failed to bring them together. The reason is, as said earlier, that too fast an external growth has given the mankind, in general, no time to look within. As a result the gulf between the external growth and the internal growth has become even wider. While the external growth may bring **'Prosperity'**, it is the internal growth which brings **'Peace'**. Unless both are taken care of simultaneously, they will always remain opposed to each other. The world today realizes that all kinds of revolutions viz. industrial, political, economic or social have failed to achieve the goal of **'Prosperity and Peace'** bringing together. Perhaps, the answer now lies in **'internal revolution'** or the **'spiritual revolution'**. It is also to be understood that it has no conflict with the earlier revolutions. It will only supplement and reinforce them.

When this balance between the external growth and the internal growth is realised, **'Peace'** will become a natural and effortless outcome. Many world problems, which have been eluding solution for a long time, will become easy to solve, as our inner boundaries expand beyond geographical boundaries. The globe would then appear to be one entity truly reflecting the message of our scriptures as described below:

अयं निजः परो वेत्ति गणना लघुचेतसाम्।
उदारचरितानां तु, वसुधैव कुटुम्बकम्॥

(Ayam Nijah Paro Vetti Garhna Laghuchetsam;
Udarcharitanam tu, Vasudhaiva Kutumbkam)

"Petty minds think—this is mine and that is others'; but for the liberal ones the entire world is one family."

Thus, the expansion of inner boundaries is what is called **'Spirituality'**. When one feels oneself as a part of the whole, he becomes spiritual and his **'self'** merges with the **'universal self'**. He is then at peace with himself and the world outside. When the whole world realizes this truth of the inevitability of co-existence, the earth would become heaven with peace all-around.

It was very exciting and a great experience to be in the UN General Assembly hall, where about 2,000 delegates had assembled from all over the world. The India delegation was the biggest with around 300 delegates. The summit went on from August 28 to 31. It was a very sublime experience to listen to the spiritual and religious leaders of the world speaking from a common platform.

While religion had always been helpful in achieving peace at an individual level, perhaps for the first time it was sought to be a tool for world peace. The message of all the speakers was more or less the same. All shared the concern for growing conflicts and emphasized the need of coming together, realizing that the entire humanity had a common connection in the form of God, whatever be name given to this entity. This realization is the epitome of spirituality. The overall experience was very enriching and broadened my vision immensely.

During this summit, on the first day itself, I got the inspiration of writing a book on "Positive Living". I wanted to put together all the cardinal principles of positive living in a concise and logical manner for the benefit of those who were not in a position to read bulky scriptures, be they of any religion. The main source of this book was to be the Bhagavad-Gita, which I consider to be a universal scripture above all religions. Gita is the only spiritual text to be authored right amidst a battlefield. Under an extremely critical situation, Lord Krishna removed all the delusions that Arjuna had, in a very systematic and convincing manner, and prepared him for a life of high endeavour. I consider Gita to be a book of science and art of life.

On my return to India, I had a discussion with my publisher about this proposed book and he encouraged it wholeheartedly. I wanted to dedicate this book to the 21st century and therefore the title chosen was *21 Laws of Positive Living*. I paid a visit to Narayanashrama Tapovanam also to meet Swamiji for his guidance about this book. Swamiji not only approved my initiative, but also took keen interest in its contents. Accordingly, 21 aspects of life were identified.

In the writing of this book, I became the first beneficiary as I had to employ all my wisdom gained so far with the blessings of Swamiji. Ultimately, the book came out to be an excellent publication and was released in the International Book Fair at Delhi in February 2002. Later, it was also placed in the World Book Fair at Denver in USA in June 2002.

This book was also translated in Hindi and other foreign languages, like Spanish and Bahasa, thus becoming an international publication. I made an appeal to the readers at the end of the book to give goodness a try and live it fully, if they wanted to make the best use of their lives.

Swamiji often says that the three most important requirements of a truly spiritual life are elegance of character, behavioural majesty and interactional excellence. These traits come to us only when we cautiously follow certain laws of life. These laws have been enumerated in this book. Since then, it has become my endeavour to live them fully. In doing so, the munificence and guidance of Swamiji has always helped me.

In the meantime, I wrote few more books. After my first book, *Positive Lessons from Life*, I kept on writing about my good experiences of life in a similar way. However, with time, the write-ups become more contemplative. The next book was *Spiritual Lessons from Life*, which contained similar lessons but with a deeper note. Later, these two books were published under the titles *Positive Mind Power* and *Positive Mind Therapy* by Sterling Publishers of Delhi.

More Writings and Books

I also wrote a book on administration, both in English and Hindi. The title of the English book was *Power of Positive Management* and its foreword was written by Shri E. Sreedharan, who himself is a close devotee of Swamiji. One more book which has been published by Sterling is *Think Positive and Things will Go Right*. In this book there are 50 events of my life in which difficult situations were sorted out by positive contemplation. In retrospect, I feel that this is the essence of spiritual power, and when we live in tune with nature with the least feeling of 'doer ship', higher powers take command of our life and steer it through. This is what I learnt from Swamiji in my long association with him.

Sterling Publishers brought out two more books of mine in subsequent years. Their titles are *The Power of Positive Words* and *The Power of Positive Anecdotes*. The foreword of the first book was written by Swamiji, which was an indication of his continued blessings and confidence in me. Both these books proved to be useful for the readers and many editions of these have come out. I translated them into Hindi also and consequently they became even more popular. Apart from eight books published by Sterling and their translations in Hindi, some miscellaneous books were also compiled by me and published by Kabir Peace Mission for promoting the cause of the Mission. The Mission encouraged many others also to write good books. The total number of books promoted or published by the Mission, crossed 50, and the process is still on.

I have mentioned this because I could never imagine that such a development would ever take place in my life. In my childhood and even later, I had been a shy person with hardly any interest in general reading or writing. Once my spiritual sprouting started and grew under the loving guidance of Swamiji, the inner resources of mine got expression in this way. This is perhaps the real purpose of spirituality. Even my oral skills improved with time and I got a large number of opportunities to speak before different gatherings on different subjects and at different places. Most of the time, I can now speak without any prior preparation. I consider all this to be the grace of God, who makes me an instrument on such occasions. Even in my writings, I feel that I only took dictation and if I were to write the same books again, perhaps it would not be possible. I feel this development was possible only because of my spiritual progress.

*****

16

Swamiji Visits Lucknow

My association with Swamiji continued as earlier--in fact it intensified. Our wish was that Swamiji visit Lucknow also and stay with us. He very kindly agreed to our request and visited Lucknow for three years consecutively in 2001, 2002 and 2003. His visits were in the month of April, which is the beginning of summer. As in Kanpur, Swamiji was very well-received in Lucknow also and left a deep mark on the people here. For the first time they came in contact with a saint who was so open, clear and practical in his teachings. For most of them it was a new dimension of spirituality which had no conflict with day to day life. On the other hand, it made their life richer as well as harmonious. Swamiji's talks on *Vivek Choodamani* and *Yog Vashistha* were a new exposure for all. The audience had never thought that so much wisdom was hidden in our scriptures that all situations of life could be tackled gracefully. However, the difficult part was the manner in which this wisdom could be converted into practice. That was where the association and guidance of a spiritual master helped.

It was everyone's wish that Swamiji's visits to Lucknow continue in the coming years also, but for many reasons it could not be possible. One reason was that my sons' problem was increasing day by day. Also, Swamiji's engagements were on the rise and he was involved in many other activities. As a result Swamiji could not come to Lucknow after 2003. Only in November 2015 did he come for the inauguration of Smriti Bhavan, of which a detailed mention will be made later.

*****

17

Administration as Sadhana

All through this period, my *sadhana* was going on in two fields. The first was the domestic and the second was my job itself, which I always considered to be a great means of self-development as well as service to society. As Principal Secretary of Medical and Health Department, I considered the patients as *Rogi-Narayana* and tried to serve them in the best possible manner. During this period the culture of the department changed greatly and this was experienced by all. Similarly, as Principal Secretary of the Prison Department, I considered the prisoners as *Bundi-Narayana* and dealt with them in that spirit. Generally, the Prison Department is known for bad incidents like suicides, quarrels and jail breaks. However, during the period of about ten months that I spent in the department, there was hardly any such incident. On the other hand, the environment in our jails became very positive. Certainly, it was on account of subtle vibrations which spread if one carries genuine good feelings for people. In this way I see a direct connection between spiritual development and administrative excellence.

In April 2005, the Government posted me as Commissioner of Lucknow Division. This is one the most important divisions of the state. This position also came to me unexpectedly. Due to my sons' movement problem, I could not go out of Lucknow. Therefore providence gave me this position at Lucknow itself. I was not elated because of the position but because of the opportunity the position provided me for serving people, and also to make more experiments with spirituality in administration. By this time my leanings were well known and I wanted to prove that real success came through only right means.

Lucknow Division consists of six big districts and has multifarious problems, but with Swamiji's grace, the administration of the whole Division went on very smoothly with full support of my team. Though there were occasional dilemmas, but providence provided timely solutions to them and I never had to make any compromise with my conscience. This is something I want to emphatically state, that the spiritual dimension of our personality is our greatest strength and protection. Today's maladministration is due to lack of this dimension and hardly anything is being done in this direction. Fortunately, saints like Swamiji are playing a big role in inculcating this dimension. The creation of FRNV (Foundation for Restoration of National Values) under the leadership of Shri E. Sreedharan is an important step in this direction. I will come to this issue later.

I held the post of Commissioner, Lucknow, for more than two years. In the State Assembly Elections of 2007, the Government in Uttar Pradesh changed and with that I was shifted to the Higher Education Department as its Principal Secretary. Here I got a great opportunity to interact with universities, educational institutions and students. All through, my belief had been that we needed to present spirituality in a scientific manner and if it is done, it will always be accepted by all. After coming in contact with Swamiji, my conviction about this reality increased even further and I have always striven to live this conviction. I can humbly claim that it has never disappointed me.

After working in the Higher Education Department, I was promoted to the post of Social Welfare Commissioner of Uttar Pradesh, a post equivalent to Chief Secretary but not institutionalized well. I silently worked there for about a year and completed some of my writings before retiring on July 31, 2009. I left the service with full satisfaction and conveyed my feelings to all my colleagues in the form of a letter. This letter was greatly appreciated and I am reproducing it here.

Rakesh Kumar Mittal   Social Welfare Commissioner
IAS   Government of Uttar Pradesh, Lucknow
Dated: 31st July, 2009

Dear Friends,

This is to share my feelings at the time of my relinquishing IAS after putting in 34 years of service. I joined this service in the year 1975 more by the dint of circumstances than by design, which resulted into my somewhat late entry into it. Since the very beginning, I have considered this service to be a great opportunity for self-development as well as for serving the society. I still maintain this belief despite many aberrations in the system over a period of time. Perhaps that has been the situation always and we have to find ways to meet them gracefully.

    Like all the members of the service, I also got opportunities to serve in various capacities and at various places. It also took me around the whole country and many countries abroad. Apart from the job experiences, such visits greatly widened my vision and increased the depth of my understanding of the people. More I travelled across the country, more I developed reverence towards our great land and I have no hesitation in saying that even at this age I know little of its diversities. I feel very satisfied to have served this land to the best of my capacity.

    This service also brought me in contact with a large number of people coming from various backgrounds and they came from all sections of the society. While a good number of them has found a place in my address diaries, countless are those who have left only good memories. Many faces visit my mind, who showed their gratefulness with a smiling face or even with tears for something done to them as a part of my duty for which I was paid adequately. But the joy of seeing their faces was something which could never be evaluated in terms of money. I consider this earning to be the real wealth of mine which will remain with me perhaps even after this life.

There have been occasional disappointments during the course of my long service but there has never been any frustration or despair. While at the time of leaving the service, there is some confusion but it is accompanied with full hope. Though one may debate over the future of our service, I have no doubt that the new generation entering the service has all the talent to set things right and the present confusion, to me, appears only a period of transition.

I have interacted with many young officers of the service closely and this is what makes me optimistic about the future. My only advice to young officers is that they should look at their career with a long term perspective and not in pieces. If they do so, short term aberrations will not bother them and they will not only be able to contribute their best to the system but will also have inner fulfilment.

I would also like to share something about my mission in future. An incident in the early years of my service impelled me to contemplate on the philosophy of life and this contemplation went for a couple of years. At the end of this I was fully convinced that life has a larger goal and every vocation is only a means to achieve that goal. From that point of view also, our service gives us greater opportunities. In order to share this conviction, I became an instrument in the creation of 'Kabir Peace Mission' with the association of few like-minded friends in the year 1990. This small plant has now grown into a strong tree with more than 2000 life members with greater vigour. In this pursuit, I shall need your help, association as well as guidance.

Overall it has been a very satisfying inning and I feel that I could not have played better. I got all the support from the system whether it was the peer group, members of the other services, public representatives, media or the common man. As mentioned earlier, I have a large number of friends from all walks of life. It is now time to know them better and to enrich life further by interacting with them. It will give a great joy to remain in touch with you. My mobile number is 94150-15859 and generally it is open at all hours. My residential address is 'UPVAN' 1/14 Vishwas Khand, Gomtinagar, Lucknow-226010 and my Email is rakesh_mittal_2000@yahoo.com.

As I close this letter, I profoundly thank you for your wonderful association during my service.

With regards and best wishes.

Yours Sincerely,
(Rakesh K. Mittal)

All members of IAS U.P. Cadre

The purpose of including this letter is to convey the fact that any profession or engagement can always be made a means of self-development. It is more so when our profession offers opportunities to serve others. Swamiji always emphasized the aspect that all those who were engaged in public service should understand spirituality even better. That is why he disseminated spiritual wisdom all through his life and continues to do so. Needless is to say that I have also been a great beneficiary of this wisdom.

*****

18

Role of Spirituality in Administration

I am touching on this subject on the specific suggestion of Swamiji. All the maladies of society which we see all around today are due to lack of spiritual dimension in our administration, be that in any field. I, myself, began my administrative career with a dilemma which was very soon resolved due to my spiritual sprouting. Thereafter, there was no confusion and I could face all the situations in life with clarity and resolve, though with occasional disappointments. Even these occasions laid the foundation for a stronger future and turned into blessings. Perhaps that is the role providence plays when we are true to ourselves.

I often recall two interactions of mine with well known administrators of this country. The first was in the year 1992 at Delhi, when I met a former ICS officer,. Shri Dharma Vira, who had occupied positions like Cabinet Secretary, Governor of West Bengal and Karnataka and many others. He was known for his firmness, competence and human touch. After listening to him for some time, when I asked him to give few words of advice for a straightforward officer, he felt very happy and gave two pieces of advice. The first was that a straightforward officer should be a dangerously honest officer. It meant that his honestly or straightforwardness

Role of Spirituality in Administration

should instil fear among the wicked and comfort among the good persons. According to him, then only honesty had a meaning. The second piece of advice was that honestly should not only mean being a stickler of rules but it should mean a positive interpretation of rules. After all, rules are made for people and not the other way round. Therefore an honest officer should always be helpful. Then only his honesty had a meaning.

Another interaction was in CIRD, Vasundhara, Ghaziabad, in November 2001 with Shri E. Sreedharan. We were attending a two-day programme organized by our Swami Bhoomanandaji. It was my first meeting with Shri E. Sreedharan though I had heard his name in many contexts. As expected, I was deeply influenced by him and while at the lunch table, I asked him the secret his success in one line. To this his response was very interesting. He said why did I need one line answer, he would give me a one word answer and this one word was "integrity". Though I knew the answer, but coming from Shri E. Sreedharan, this word carried a lot of meaning. Thereafter I contemplated on this word several times and realized that it was not one word but it was a text book in itself and that too on "life".

These two interactions show that an honest life is a great mission in itself and it becomes more so when practiced in public life. Fortunately I was already on that path and these interactions only reinforced my faith and conviction. The question is how to imbibe these qualities. They do not come to us from mundane text books, they come only by divine grace and when one seeks them. Those who are fortunate to be such seekers, soon realize that it is always a winning situation, though it may not appear so apparently. No situation in life, then, appears frightening because there is always a firm faith in the law of nature which, in short, is that we reap only what we sow

There have been many instances when a difficult situation got solved by providence with no embarrassment to anybody. It happens only when there is complete guilelessness and detachment. If so, why should there be a doubt about the practicability of honesty in worldly life? The catch is that honesty has to be integrated. Even if we slip in one aspect of life, it has an adverse effect and we suffer accordingly. Therefore, effort should always to fill up the gaps and make one's personality as integrated as possible. This is what we call *Spiritual Sadhana*. A Sadguru is a great help in this regard and it may not be wrong to say that without him, it is not possible.

Today, despite all the physical developments, due to lack of ethics and moral values, the society faces untold miseries. The administrative set-up, be it political, judicial or administrative, which is supposed to take care of this misery, is itself adding salt to the wound. Their sensitivity is getting lost fast, as a result of which even the people are losing their patience. This is the cause of various agitations which often turn violent. My experience as an administrator has been that the inner state of mind of the administrator has tremendous impact on the environment. It I work with integrity with everybody's welfare in mind, it has a cascading effect and problems are sorted out amicably in a peaceful manner. In such a situation everyone turns out to be a winner and happiness prevails all around.

Thus we find that spirituality has a direct role in good administration. It is an indication of ignorance to say that there is a conflict between the two. On the other hand, they complement each other. I can say with full conviction that my spiritual exposition always helped me in dealing with various administrative problems. In the society we live in today, some adjustments are always required but not compromise with principles. There has been no occasion in my career where I had to act against my conscience, though at times I had to act against my wish. This kind of adjustment is required in all aspects of life and administration is no exception.

Time has now come when society at large has to understand the genesis of prevailing maladies and address them in the right way. The socio-spiritual forces have also to play their role in this background. The religion and spirituality have to play very important roles, provided they are in right hands. Swamiji has been playing this role for decades but much more has to be done. Let all those who are fortunate to have understood life in true perspective also contribute their mite in this direction.

*****

19

Journey after Retirement

I had no specific plan after retirement and left it to nature to decide for me. It was not a passive surrender but a very positive faith in providence. I was well established in Lucknow, with a comfortable financial and social status. I had no craze for any post-retirement position. Moreover, I could not move out of Lucknow because of family reasons. I think providence took all these factors into account and provided me many opportunities which kept me busy, happy and fulfilled. These came in sequence and effortlessly. As mentioned in my retirement letter, my interaction with friends increased and became more meaningful. Many of them, for whom my official position was a constraint earlier, felt more at ease with me. All these developments kept on enriching my life further and the process is still on. My daily routine goes on as it used to earlier and has become even more disciplined. I consider all this to be a result of my Master's grace and inner development.

Departure of Amit

Coming back to the chain of events at home, my elder son Amit's problem was increasing day by day but his enthusiasm was intact. He still hoped that he would get cured. Soon before my retirement, he got promoted as Assistant Manager in SIDBI which entitled him for many

Journey after Retirement

perks. He used to feel very happy about it though he was hardly a beneficiary of them. My younger son, Rohit, who had started a small enterprise in the year 2003, more as a pastime, was finding it difficult to continue it. As a result, this venture had to be closed within one year of my retirement. The physical problem of both of them was increasing and a good amount of our time used to be spent in their care as well as company. Even this situation was enriching us and regular interaction with Swamiji was a great help in mitigating our occasional afflictions.

In the beginning of 2013, Amit had started giving up. He gave hints to this effect in a note dated January 4, 2013. It was evident from his body language also. In February, when I was to go out of Lucknow for a few days, for the first time he wanted me not to go and I heeded to his wish. During the *Holi* festival, he did not come out of the house, something that he had never done before. In the first week of April, when Swamiji came to CIRD, Delhi, I had a meeting with him and shared the situation at length with him. Swamiji listened to me attentively and after a brief pause asked me whether I was prepared for Amit's departure. With tears in my eyes I gave my assent. Then he asked me whether my wife was also ready, to which I expressed my affirmation. After this, Swamiji himself talked to my wife over phone and appeared satisfied. He did not say anything after that but his studied silence conveyed the inevitable message along with his blessings.

On May 3, 2013, when Amit came from office, he decided to proceed on leave. He was finding it difficult to spend the day there and we were in agreement with him. May 4 and 5 being holidays, I moved an application to his office with a medical certificate on Monday, May 6. He became very introspective during this period as if he had a premonition of the events to come. He asked me to call his cousin (my brother's son) and advised his mother to provide him white bedding as well as clothes. On the night of 7, he went to bed earlier than his usual time and appeared to be calmer than he used to be. Though a bit surprised, we also retired to our bedroom. In the morning when we got up at about 5:15 a.m. Amit was no more. According to the doctor, the end had come a little before.

We took the development with calmness and fortitude. Amit's cousin was to arrive the same morning and he did. I informed all my close relatives and friends, many of whom arrived from outside to attend the cremation planned for the evening. We also decided to donate Amit's eyes and arrangements were made for that. Throughout the day, I attended to a large number of visitors as well as phone calls. My wife also remained very composed and attended to all the visitors in a serene manner. After the cremation in the evening, I declared there itself that Amit was a great soul and instead of any mourning, there would be a homage meet after two days. A large number of friends and well-wishers were present on both the occasions. Everyone felt enriched, though with a heavy heart, amid the prevailing mood. I was able to address the gathering during the homage with a lot of equanimity and gave the full background of Amit's journey.

How could this happen? It did not happen in a day. It was my Guru's *Sannidhi*, which had nurtured me and my wife in such a sublime manner. Was it our spiritual dimension, which kept us so balanced in one of the worst moments of life or just a blessing of our spiritual master? These are the issues which the readers of this book may talk about, but for me the greatest blessing in life is to take its events with equanimity. Swamiji mentioned this in his letters and also emphasized upon the perishability of objective world events, be they pleasant or unpleasant. This constant refrain in Swamiji's teachings has helped us in transcending the effect of worldly events to a great extent. Is it not a supreme achievement of spiritual awakening, which comes only when we are under the care of an enlightened soul? As a support to this claim, I produce my letter, dated May 20, 2013, which I wrote to Swamiji.

Date: 20.05.2013

Rev. Swamiji
Pranams.

I could not speak to you on 13th May but we all kept remembering you. Surely the programmes in the Ashrama must have gone very well.

Amit's condolences are over on 19.05.13 (Sunday). With your grace, God has given us enough strength to bear the situation elegantly. It is more than 20 years now that you came in our life and reinforced it with spiritual wisdom. We could live with the problem mainly on account of this.

Amit's end came so peacefully that we wonder on the plan of nature. Last month when we met at CIRD Vasundhara, we talked on this subject and you blessed for his peaceful end. The same came so true.

We now look upon your guidance and blessing for future so that Amit's departure becomes meaningful. I would also like to meet you in person at earliest possible.

Aruna is conducting herself with strength and this in itself, is a great relief.

Our pranams to Ma and Naya Swamiji.

Humbly Yours
Rakesh K. Mittal

The response to this letter came in the form of a message which Swamiji sent, for a souvenir proposed to be brought out in Amit's memory. Very soon I started working on this with the help of my niece, who could share my feelings to a great extent. The purpose was twofold. The first was to preserve relevant material related to Amit's memories at one place and the second was to divert our attention from bereavement in a constructive manner. This souvenir, which was titled as "Memories of Amit" (Amit *ki Smritiyaan*), was prepared in less than three months after his departure and was released in a very solemn manner on July 27, 2013. The hall was full of friends and *Hindustan Times*, Lucknow covered the event in a very dignified manner, under the title, "Making a Difference". Its text is quoted below:

> It was a book release function with a difference.
>
> It also was a tribute paying ceremony but with a difference. Retired bureaucrat Rakesh Mittal, 64, organized a book release at The Brahmakumaris' Atma Chintan Bhavan, Gomtinagar on Saturday evening. The book was 'Memories of Amit' published by Rakesh in memory of his son Amit. Brahmakumari's centre in charge Brahmakumari Radha released the book.
>
> The hall was full of people and none ever witnessed a father paying tribute to a son in this manner. Brahmakumari Radha wrote in the book: 'I had heard about birth celebration or wedding celebration. But first time ever in life I witnessed a celebration of passing away.' She wrote this recollection about the May 10 ceremony that Rakesh held two days after Amit passed away. That ceremony and Saturday's book release ceremony tried to look and show the people spiritual aspects of life and death.
>
> Amit, at 18, was discovered having an incurable disease called 'Hereditary Spastic Paraparesis', in which nervous system of the patient degenerates gradually and the average age of such person is 35 years. Amit passed away few months before his 40th birthday.
>
> At the book release Rakesh spoke about Amit's life between his birth and his death. He talked about how Amit despite knowing his fate, was extra ordinarily passionate about life, experiencing, relationships, family, learning or working.
>
> The book has Amit's pictures at different stages of life until few months before his death. It also has letters that Amit wrote to his father, to mother and some letters that the father and the mother wrote back, certificates of several of his achievements, recollections about him by friends and relatives, condolence messages on his passing away.
>
> All those who attended the book release event, got a copy of the book that anyway has no cover price on it.
>
> - HT CITY

The souvenir began with the message of Swamiji, which is produced below:

1st June 2013

Amit Mittal

Hari Om Tat Sat. Whenever I used to think of Amit and Rohit, the first and second son of Rakesh Mittal and Aruna, instantly would spring forth immense fondness, concern, anxiety and a strange note of suspense. The manner in which both Aruna and Rakesh looked after Amit, providing all the medical care as well as personal attention is quite rare. Rakesh had lovingly taken Amit to the distinguished hospitals in the country and also centres outside, seeking redress, a step not always within the reach of many parents!

Amit suffered from a tormenting condition called Hereditary Spastic Paraparesis, something not common. The boy was then just 14; intelligent, diligent and good in his performance. To come to know that such a good boy was becoming a victim to an incurable medical condition, known to grow increasingly worse every day, was alarming, disheartening and enfeebling. But there was no time to honour these emotions and allow them to take over the mind.

Aruna on her motherly front and Rakesh on the fatherly role, lovingly, hopefully and fervently did everything possible. Amit was helped to find a job in 1996 in SIDBI, Uttar Pradesh, which he held on even moving on a wheel chair. His work was good and he was promoted as Asstt. Manager. The muscles continued to grow weaker and weaker, disabling movements, step by step. Ultimately it affected the respiratory muscles too, which led to Amit's final disembodiment.

Rakesh came to me many years back in New Delhi, when I was hosted by Balan Subramanian in Hauz Khas. Before long, he and Aruna had Brahmavidya Deeksha from me. Ever since, both their children also crept into my heart with a special note of fond concern. Their welfare was equally my concern. I used to have regular discussions with Rakesh and Aruna on the sons' health and wellbeing.

It is certainly unfortunate to have any such physical disadvantage in the family. But the whole world is a game in the hands of Providence. We can at best witness its movements and outcomes. Despite the grave uncertainty and conflict, it is a fortune to have an occasion to express persisting fondness, as Rakesh and Aruna have displayed for decades.

Human mind has enough potential, possibility, to assimilate any impact from the interactional world. Once assimilated, everything becomes enrichment. I think this is what verily transpired in the life of this blessed couple.

Amit was very fortunate in this. In having given him such amazing care, fondness and partnership, both Rakesh and Aruna deserve all appreciation and regard.

While Rakesh had his exacting Administrative Tasks, of varying dimensions and importance, to keep him engrossed, Aruna had always to be physically close to Amit, sharing his plight, needs, difficulties and pressures. May be the spiritual seeking and association it brought right from the start have stood in good stead with them, making their attention to Amit not alone a mere fulfilment of need or compulsion, but also an elevational interaction and enlightenment.

Vasishtha Deva's words to Rama are apt for the occasion.

शून्यमाकीर्णतामेति मृत्युरप्युत्सवायते।
आपत्सम्पदिवाभाति विद्वज्जनसमागमे।।

Shoonyam-aakeernataam-eti mrityurapi-utsavaayate
Aapat-sampad-ivaabhaati vidvajjana-saMagame

Void becomes full, death turns into festivity, calamity transforms into fortune, when the Enlightened arrive on the scene and interact with the afflicted.

I have often thought of the parents and their children very specially. May Amit's disembodiment give them additional enrichment and a great insight into the complexities of Nature as also the astounding radiance of the Spirit, the Soul, which ever remains unaffected and full. Love and *ashirvaad* to the entire family.

Antaraatma,
Swami Bhoomananda Tirtha

Overall, this souvenir became a book of inspiration for all those who face such afflictions in life. In this I also included an interview which the *Hindustan Times* took on Father's Day in June 2013. The interview was mainly against the background of Amit's death and covered my views about the whole development. Since I feel it to be relevant to my spiritual journey, this interview is also being produced here.

An Interview of Shri Rakesh Mittal on Father's Day

(Appeared in *Hindustan Times*, Lucknow on 16.6.2013)

'While living he was my son, while leaving he became my master ......'

That's how Rakesh Kumar Mittal, 64, a gritty and inspiring man sums up his life as a father.

"I am writing the memoir of Amit", says the well-known IAS officer who is equally popular in his retirement days, as we begin the conversation.

On May 8, Amit Mittal passed away in his sleep at their Vishwas Khand residence in Lucknow's Gomtinagar, a few months before his 40th Birthday.

"My wife Aruna's words that Amit's birth was a good omen proved true. Shortly after his birth, I cracked the Civil Services exam." Mittal recalls.

"We used to do horse riding together when he was five," he says with a faint smile. Everything was normal until Amit (after having some health problems, at the age of 18 was taken to the All India Institute of Medical Science (AIIMS), Delhi, where he was detected with 'Hereditary Spastic Paraparesis'.

"The doctors told us that it was an incurable hereditary condition in which the nervous system degenerates gradually and the average age of such patients is 35 years. I took him to many health centres, including the ones abroad, but the prediction was the same everywhere," he shares.

This was the background in which Amit and his family had to spend their life.

"But there was no decline in Amit's enthusiasm. He was a brilliant student. However, pursuing studies in the normal way was not possible for him anymore. He took admission in an open university (IGNOU) and passed out with flying colours," say Mittal with fatherly pride.

"Amit's fate was decided. We only wanted to see him happy, and he never let us down. He faced it all with dignity. In 2008, Amit was to turn 35. My wife donated a cow to the Bhoothnath temple in Indira Nagar. That cow is still there and we go to see it. Nature had been preparing us for the final result." Amit's disabilities had been increasing gradually – from 50% to 75% to 90%.

In 1996, the Small Industrial Development Bank of India (SIDBI), Lucknow gave him a job. In 1998, Amit fell down in his room and broke his legs. He had to be on leave for six months and his office fully cooperated with him. After this, he permanently took to the wheel chair.

"But despite the odds he continued to dream of higher education, foreign trips and marriage and made efforts to fulfil those dreams. He did a web designing course through correspondence and even attempted MCA and MBA, but his body failed him." Mittal tells HT City.

But this is only half of Mittal's story as a super-father. On turning 18, his other son, Rohit, too was detected with the same condition and fate as his brother.

"Amit's Passing away has affected Rohit psychologically. The two were constant partners," says the doting father.

Nature's grand design

Mittal knows his strengths. His spiritual energies not only saw him through but also acted as the driving force behind the courage his wife and sons showed.

'The man, who retired in 2009 as commissioner Social Welfare, got inclined towards spirituality and life's philosophies in the age of 31. "After transfer from a post, my associates held a farewell dinner for me. A friend commented –'You worked so hard and so honestly on that job, but such people have to regret in the end'. I was taken aback at the comment. I started thinking as to why one should be good. Was there any science of goodness? I set out on a quest. Since my quest was genuine, nature began providing opportunities – through books, friends and experience – to find the answers.

Mittal has been a man of science. Before entering Civil Services he had been topper in the Indian Institute of Technology (IIT), Roorkee right from the beginning. "I was spiritually inclined but always looked upon religion with contempt. I was a keen observer of people and noticed that many outwardly religious people were not religious from within," he says.

Until they turned 18, both the kids of Rakesh and Aruna Mittal were normal – physically and mentally. They ran, played tennis, and went horse riding. "No one takes it (such tragic news) gladly. It is not that we don't cry and weep or do not shed tears now. We do. But the tears are transitory. We don't persist in them. Everyone's biggest joys and sorrows are secret / private," he says with moist eyes yet in a soft and firm voice.

After a brief pause, Mittal further says, "It is all a very logical design or conspiracy of nature. It is just and rational. You cannot question it. Nature designed it that way. Perhaps, I was chosen to be Amit and Rohit's father for I would be most suited to them. Perhaps my spirituality, thinking and attitude were all aligned in a predestined manner."

"How else do you explain that a year before the detection of Amit's ailments, I founded the Kabir Peace Mission. I thought I became clear in my spiritual conviction and wanted to share it with others. So I founded the mission to develop positive thinking in our society. We might not be able to change everything, but are making inputs towards change," says the 1975 batch IAS officer.

The mission's motto is 'Curse not darkness, Light a lamp', "*Kyakashta* (what sorrow?). There are some people who don't have children. There are others who don't marry. There are some who lose their children in accidents or mishaps. Why should I make myself a subject of pity?

Sitting in his Kabir Peace Mission office, he says, "We often try to rise above dukha (sorrows) and seek sukha (happiness). The trick is to rise above both sukha and dukha. That's the state of life one should seek."

Just the other day a friend came to see Mittal. "He had lost his son in the Kargil war. I told him – "We should not grieve the passing away of our respective sons."

(Interviewed by Mr. Pankaj Jaiswal)

While the above may create an impression that a person with spiritual wisdom becomes a man with a heart of stone, it is far from true. The fact is that a spiritually wise person is even more sensitive to outer stimulations than a normal person. The difference is that he is not carried away by them and responds with equanimity. He is equally affected by their nature but does not react knowing their transitory nature. At times, there may be outwardly responses from him but inwardly he gets enriched and sublimated by all the events of life. To be candid, tears rolled out of my eyes on several occasions in life and it happened very frequently in the case of Amit's demise also, but always a new inspiration dawned. This only added to my resolve to live even more elegantly. If so, is not spiritual wisdom the highest treasure to be cherished by everyone?

Departure of Rohit

Now I come to the story of my younger son Rohit. As has been mentioned several times earlier, he was also suffering from the same disease as his elder brother. The impact of the disease was even more on him as he could see his elder brother's condition deteriorating with time. This affected him in ways more than one. Firstly, he could not concentrate on his studies. Secondly, he had become very introverted and at times irritable also. All these factors brought about a faster deterioration in him. Though he did not speak much, it was quite evident that he used to think a lot about this matter. The death of his elder brother in May 2013 shook him completely and he became extremely quiet. Soon it became a matter of concern and by September it had become clear that he would not live long. Doctors advised us to protect him from infections, but it was exactly what happened in the month of October. His condition became bad in the morning of October 15, and he was immediately shifted to the ICU in the hospital. The doctors tried their best to check the spreading infection, but failed to do so. Rohit passed away in the early hours of October 16, 2013.

Again, I and my wife faced the situation with great calm. I informed all my close friends and relatives and arranged for Rohit's eyes donation also. This time I was a little selective in informing them because I didn't want to spread panic. While we ourselves were calm, all those who learnt of this news were extremely shocked and regarded us as being unfairly treated by life. I wanted to avoid this unnecessary pity or feeling of injustice to us. Despite all the shock it gave to us, I had full faith in nature's justice which again was due to the grace of our spiritual master. I informed Swamiji also and took his blessings. All the ceremonies were again conducted in a serene manner. A prayer meeting was arranged after three days of cremation and representatives of all the faiths attended the same. Again, it was a sublime occasion for all those who attended the meeting.

Our lives changed completely after the departure of both our sons. While we felt that both the souls had had their peaceful end, their physical absence haunted us frequently, if not all the time. Whenever it now happens, their physical difficulty also visits our mind and we feel relieved about their trauma ending. Both of them were pure souls who never hurt anyone and always tried to be good to others. We never noticed any anger, jealousy or greed in them. The question of any ego did not even arise. Departure of such souls in so peaceful a manner always gives us the feeling as if we are the special parents who nature chose for bringing them up. We don't want to present ourselves as ordinary parents suffering from the bodily separation from our children. On the other hand, we want to give a positive meaning to this cosmic drama so that even this adversity could become meaningful.

*****

20

Smriti Bhavan

When the problem of Amit and Rohit had begun, some friends used to relate it to our residence at Lucknow and often advised us to shift. While I never believed in such a solution, on the persistence of my wife I agreed to look for another piece of land. For this I sold my ancestral property in my hometown and applied to the Lucknow Development Authority (LDA) for a piece of land in Amit's name. A good piece of land was allotted to him in the year 2005, when I was the Commissioner of Lucknow and also the Chairman of LDA. At one good location LDA had allotted 28 plots, out of which one was given to Amit under the handicapped quota. While I was planning construction on this plot, a Public Interest Litigation (PIL) was filed in the Supreme Court, alleging irregularities in the allotment process. The court ordered the maintenance of status quo and the process came to a halt. In a way I felt relieved as I never wanted to change my residence. As a result, things continued as they were.

After about seven years, in August 2012, the court declared the allotments valid. By this time, it was too late to think of construction as the condition of Amit had become quite bad. The matter, therefore, remained pending and we had no time to think of any plan with regard to this piece of land. After the demise of Amit and Rohit, our attention was drawn to this issue and I started thinking of possibilities.

The price of the land had increased substantially during this period. However, the selling option was never in our mind as we wanted to use this land for a good purpose. The manner in which it could be done was a subject of considered decision.

Several options came to our mind and I discussed them with close friends and well-wishers. Firstly, we thought of creating a new trust in the memory of our sons, but then it was decided to make use of the Kabir Peace Mission's platform. It was decided by the trustees that a building be constructed on the plot which could be used for social and spiritual activities of the Mission, as well as for activities of other like-minded organizations. This idea was somewhat on the lines of CIRD (Centre for Inner Resources Development), established by Swamiji at various places. Accordingly, the plans were prepared with this objective in mind. All through this process I was in consultation with Swamiji, whose blessings were constantly guiding me. But I needed his firm "yes" before going ahead with the project.

Our wish was to start the project on May 8, 2014, the first death anniversary of Amit. Against this background, I met Swamiji in the first week of April 2014 at CIRD Ghaziabad. Swamiji keenly saw the plans and after due consideration gave his consent to go ahead. He also accepted my request to inaugurate the building, proposed to be completed in November 2015. This building was to be named Smriti Bhavan.

Accordingly, preparations were made to start the project on May 8, 2014. A young Muslim contractor agreed to construct the building on a turnkey basis at reasonable rates, which included both material and labour charges. Initially, there were some differences with him but very soon he realized our pious intentions behind the project. Thereafter, he dedicated himself towards its timely completion. We wanted to complete the building as well as its furnishings before inauguration, for which Swamiji fixed the date of November 25, 2015. It was the day of *Kartik Poornima*, which is a very auspicious day. These details have been given only to indicate that nature co-operates with us when we undertake any pursuit selflessly for the larger good. Such resolves are also the result of spiritual clarity.

A few words about the funding of the project will also be appropriate here. As mentioned earlier, the money for land had come from the sale of my ancestral property. In this way, our ancestors participated in the project. Amit had got about Rs. 50 lakhs as various benefits after his death. Rohit and his mother owned two shops at Lucknow, where he had started his small venture earlier. Just before his death the sale of these two shops brought another Rs. 50 lakhs to us. Initially, we had planned to spend Rs. 100 lakhs in construction, which eventually rose to Rs. 125 lakhs. The rest of the amount was spent from our savings. The important point to be made here is that after spending all this money, instead of feeling impoverished we felt even more enriched. This is how nature takes care of our noble resolves.

Swamiji made a three day programme to Lucknow to inaugurate Smriti Bhavan. He came with Ma Gurupriya and many devotees. This honour conferred on us gave us great joy. Everything was arranged nicely and on the day of the inauguration, the hall was more than full. On this occasion, Swamiji spoke on the subject "Equanimity in Life". Initiating his talk, Swamiji spoke in detail about our association and how deeply concerned he had been for our welfare since the beginning. Referring to Amit and Rohit, he said that the ultimate outcome was known to him right from the first day, but he was preparing us for graceful acceptance of the reality. He felt fully satisfied with our response to the situation, an observation, which gave us a feeling of great contentment. Swamiji also appreciated the way we paid our tribute to our sons in the form of Smriti Bhavan. According to him, working towards the dissemination of spiritual wisdom was the greatest service to society.

Speaking on the subject of equanimity, Swamiji explained the nature of the mind and said that it could be regulated by the intellect. Once a person comes to realize the transitory nature of worldly events, he starts rising above them and gains equanimity in increasing measure. He extensively quoted from the Bhagvad Gita and Yoga Vashistha Ramayana, to make his point understood well. The audience listened to him attentively, and felt immensely benefitted. During his address, Swamiji also raised some socio-political issues of the country and called upon the audience to take interest in them in order to make a more harmonious and progressive society. He also said that India was the only country capable of leading the world on the strength of its cultural and spiritual values. The need was to explain them in the right manner.

Next day, many important persons of the city came to see Swamiji and discussed matters of personal as well as general interest. I, being present for most of the time, was a great beneficiary of these discussions. During this period, the idea of writing a book on my association with Swamiji came to my mind. This was subsequently approved Swamiji when we visited the Ashrama in February-March, 2016. Our association was to become 25 years old in October-November 2016 and I thought of completing this book by that time. If it has fructified, it is again a blessing of my *Sadguru*.

During his stay in Lucknow, we had a chance to speak on many matters, personal as well as social. In one of the personal conversations, Swamiji hinted that both Amit and Rohit have been liberated after their death. This was something very assuring, as we also used to think on these lines. Swamiji's assurance in this regard removed all traces of bereavement from our minds and we felt blessed in giving birth to such souls. As I stated in my interview with *Hindustan Times* after Amit's death, Amit was my son before death, but now he was my master. This belief of mine got further strengthened after Swamiji's words. The intention here is not to highlight something personal, but it is to say that life has a purpose, and if the purpose has been achieved, its length has no meaning. It has been rightly said that, "it is not so

Smriti Bhavan

important how much you live, but more important is how you live." We felt assured that Amit and Rohit both had lived well, realizing the ultimate goal of life.

Swamiji and other guests returned to CIRD, Delhi, after their inspiring visit to Lucknow. Smriti Bhavan felt charged and purified after hosting Swamiji, Ma and his other disciples. We decided to hold a weekly *satsang* every Thursday evening and it started gathering momentum soon. The format of the *satsang*, being interactive, created interest in all the participants and is going on successfully. Other programmes are also being introduced gradually. A medical consultation room has been provided for free homeopathic, allopathic and psychological treatments. This is in a nascent stage, but I am sure that in future it will serve an important purpose as Swamiji's blessings are with it.

Having made the Smriti Bhavan functional, both of us visited Mumbai and Thrissur in February-March 2016. At Mumbai, we were to pay our respects to some deities before whom we had wished timely completion of the project when we visited them in September 2014. The purpose of visiting Thrissur was to be at Narayanashrama Tapovanam for few days, express our gratitude to Swamiji and get further guidance for life. During this period my niece, Sandhya, also came to the Ashrama for the first time. In the company of Swamiji, she and I drew the outline of this book and the writing began soon after. Our plan was to get the book released by Swamiji, when he visited CIRD, Delhi in October-November 2016.

Is it not a spiritual wonder that all these plans materialized into reality?

With this, the book comes to an end as far my story is concerned. But, to say that my spiritual journey has also come to an end will not be correct. When I look within, I find many areas of improvement which I am striving to achieve. But certainly, as a result of my Guru-Sannidhi and self contemplation, life is much more harmonious. I hardly have any worldly desires or expectations from others. I try my best to perform my duty towards others and find it immensely rewarding. To me, the attainment of spiritual wisdom is the highest achievement of life. Those who tread this path are fortunate in the real sense. My only pursuit now is to share this conviction with others and nature has equipped me sufficiently to do so. I need my master's grace and goodwill of my friends to achieve this goal to the extent I can, as an instrument of God or nature, whatever we may call it.

*****

21

Inference

Having written the story of my spiritual journey, I would like to draw its inference in brief. I found human life to be a precious gift of God and a rare privilege. The goal of human life is to achieve divinity and for this nature has equipped us with the power of thinking as well as the power of discrimination. This is what differentiates human being from other creatures of nature. We have a body, a mind, an intellect, and a spirit. We have to develop all of them in order to achieve the ultimate goal. This may or may not happen in one life, but the progress can always be expedited. The sooner this reality is understood, the better it is.

The role of a "Guru" or "Master" is very important in this respect. He is the one who expedites this process. Nature plans the events of our life in such a manner that we are led to our goal if we co-operate with it. The fact is that being part of nature is progress in the real sense, while distancing from it is regression. The trick is that what appears pleasant (*preyas*) is normally not beneficent (*shreyas*). And what is beneficent (*shreyas*) does not appear pleasant (*preyas*). We have to develop this discrimination through the process of contemplation. This is where a spiritual guide helps us. A master comes to our life when we need him and are ripe to follow him.

I have also learnt that no event of life is by chance. They all are a result of a very logical process for a purpose. We should never consider any event as either "favour" or "disfavour" of nature. Nature is incapable of interfering in this process. It only ensures that we reap what we have sown. In this way we all are divine architects of our lives. In other words, we are our best friends and also the worst enemies. Once this becomes clear, all our complaints against others or our environment cease and the focus of our attention becomes "self". Then it also dawns upon us that we live in an interdependent and inter-connected cosmos. When we talk of a "Super Power" or "God" or "Nature", it only implies that there is something common in all the creations of nature. The name given to this common entity by different people may be different, but the essence and the intention is the same. When we see the world around us with this common factor in mind, love and compassion becomes a very natural phenomenon.

Now I come to the various components of human personality as mentioned earlier. The first is our body, which has to be cared for properly. Through a proper routine and food, it has to be kept healthy. We play a very important role in this respect. Though the body stops growing after a certain age, it still continues to play an important role in other dimensions of our personality. The next component is our mind which controls the sense organs. A positive mind keeps them in check, while a negative one lets them wander. A well regulated mind is, therefore, necessary for attaining the goal of life. Thus, the mental dimension of our personality is more important than the physical dimension. The same is the case with the next dimension, which we call "intellectual" dimension. It is our intellect which regulates our mind and makes it follow a certain set of values. Only a person who lives a value based life is able to graduate into the next dimension of personality called "spiritual".

The spiritual dimension of our personality transcends all the three and raises us above the trivial incidences of life. Here comes the real role of a spiritual master, who guides us on this path in his own way. Having reached this stage, equanimity dawns effortlessly and happiness or harmony with the environment is a natural outcome. However, though easily said, it is a rare fortune to reach this stage. In my study of a large number of biographies, I noticed that only a few persons reached this stage. As a result, most people leave this world sadly. The fact is that reaching this stage has no necessary connection with worldly greatness, which may be even a hindrance rather than a help. Spiritual wisdom is a prerogative of all who strive to seek it, irrespective of their worldly status. I believe that most of the time this attainment is not visible to the outer world. India is a land full of such persons who have reached that level.

In this book, I have narrated a large number of events of my life; the purpose is not to make my life known to others. The real purpose is to say that events just take place in our life and they are not planned most of the time. We attribute them to ourselves because of the false notion of "doer ship". Once this is understood, we neither resist any events nor crave for any. They are accepted as such without any judgment, with full faith in the course of nature or providence. Someone has rightly said that the journey of life is like the journey of a dead dry leaf on the mercy of divine wind. My life is presented here just like a case study, only because it has been different from a usual model of life. I have seen the best and also the worst in my life. Someone may envy it or someone may pity it, but who can judge it objectively? However, I am convinced that life has been fair to me and I could not have lived it better.

Who guided me on this path of life, either covertly or openly? Here comes the role of my spiritual guides. The urge to seek came to me in 1980 and a decade later I came in association with my spiritual master, Swami Bhoomananda Tirtha. I do not know what he noticed in me and my wife that he immediately agreed to initiate us. Swamiji also influenced us so much at our first meeting itself that we felt very assured under his care. Thus his association was a great guidance at a crucial point of our life.

In this book, I have included some correspondence with Swamiji. The purpose is to show that a living master can be our friend, guide and philosopher, all at one time. If a person is true and sincere to the master, he or she can be at ease with him. At the same time, a *Sadguru* keeps a vigilant watch on you and his words, gestures or hints should always be taken in all seriousness. I have found my association with Swamiji always enriching and sublime. His insistence on characteral elegance, behavioural majesty and interactional excellence has been a constant *mantra* of my life. This made me a great beneficiary, both in the internal as well as the external world.

This clarity dawned upon me as a result of *Guru Sannidhi*. It also induced me to pen down my thoughts in the form of various books from time to time. I have always felt that the words came to me in a flow by divine grace and I assimilated them into books. If I were to write these books again, perhaps it would be difficult to do so. It only shows that our talents are the gift of nature and if we keep this fact in mind, we shall never be the victim of any false ego.

These were some of the points I wish to share at the end of this book. I once again hope that this book will inspire many to understand spirituality in right perspective, and motivate them to walk on this path under right guidance. If this happens, this effort of mine will be amply rewarded.

Hari Om Tat Sat!

*****

About Swamiji and His Mission

Swami Bhoomananda Tirtha was born on May 13, 1933, at Parlikkad, Thrissur district in Kerala, India. During his professional life in Kolkata, he met his Guru, Baba Gangadhara Paramahamsa of Dakshin Khanda (West Bengal).The association eventually led to his introduction to the world of spirituality.

Having embraced Sanyasa at the young age of 23, Swamiji has been disseminating Brahmavidya — the knowledge of the Immortal Soul — with rare clarity, practicality and openness for the past 60 years. His rational exposition of the science of Self-knowledge and its application in the art of enriching and elevating human mind, has inspired and benefitted countless seekers, professionals, householders and students in India and abroad.

An Eloquent Speaker

A versatile scholar, a fluent and analytical speaker in English, Malayalam, Tamil, Sanskrit, Hindi and Bengali, Swamiji has literally brought the Upanishadic Wisdom of the forest hermitage to the modern metropolis. His words strike the modern rational with stunning clarity and inspire the earnest seeker instantly. As a true *Jivanmukta* (liberated while living), Swamiji strongly feels:

- There is a widespread misunderstanding that spiritual pursuit is meant only for the old and the recluse. The vast treasure of inner resources that can be harnessed by anyone to achieve excellence in any walk of life remains unnoticed due to sheer ignorance. Did not Krishna invoke the Upanishadic Wisdom in the war field of Kurukshetra to enable Arjuna fight the righteous war successfully? Far from taking man away from the world, the pursuit of the "subject wisdom" makes him an adept in whatever field he is involved.

- *Sanyasa* is wrongly regarded as a mystic wandering life. In truth, *Sanyasa* stands for exclusive dedication to the pursuit and dissemination of knowledge. *Sanyasins* in our land were like moving universities—disseminating spiritual and value education throughout the country. They did it out of their inner urge to work for the welfare of the world. They never looked for any remuneration or reward. The mightiest educative literature like Ramayana and Mahabharata, which forged the cultural backbone of the entire Bharat, came from Sanyasins and Ascetics.

- The abode of a Sanyasin—an Ashrama—must verily be a centre of learning. Its mission should be to expose people to their own Subject dimension and its unlimited potential. That would promote better understanding of the science of life and ensure for the society long term prosperity and advancement. This would set right the alarming aberration caused by the inadequate modern education system and over-indulgent materialism.

Narayanashrama Tapovanam

In order to give expression to these feelings, Swamiji founded Narayanashrama Tapovanam in 1963 on the eastern slope of Pandavagiri, about 8 km from Thrissur town in Kerala. Swamiji started living there in a small hutment, which subsequently grew into the present abode of learning. Today this ashrama is a well-known place of Kerala where devotees and seekers come from all parts of the world to seek spiritual wisdom.

As more and more people were exposed to the great benefits of this pursuit, some with larger social dimension wanted the same benefits to be reached to many others in their towns and cities. Thus was born the concept of "Jnaana Yajna"—a few weeks of exclusive learning programmes consisting of a series of public discourses, special invited talks in educational and professional institutions, as well as the rare opportunity of direct personal interaction with the realized Master every day. Annual Jnaana Yajnas in Jamshedpur and Delhi have now touched 52nd and 43rd year, respectively.

People's urge to know more and more about Brahmavidya and to pursue the path of introspection made Swamiji travel widely in India, Malaysia, Singapore, USA, Canada, UK, and Muscat. On one hand, he became well known for his compelling and incisive presentation of Gita, Upanishads, Shreemad Bhaagavatam, Yoga-Vasishtha and other Vedantic literature, while on the other, greater interaction with professional institutions made him think seriously about their increasing interest in Brahmavidya and its application to the administrative and managerial field.

Center for Inner Resources Development (CIRD)

As a result of all this, the need for a permanent center in or near Delhi was felt and thus was established the Center for Inner Resources Development (CIRD) in Vasundhara, near Delhi, in the year 2000. CIRD is now the base for Swamiji's dissemination activities in and around the capital of India. It functions in the spirit of an Ashrama—an abode of learning and growing with value orientation in the close company of the Teacher. In due course, similar centres have come up in the town of Jamshedpur in India, and Kuala Lumpur in Malaysia. All the centres are now fully functional and performing the task of spiritual dissemination as well as other activities. The Smriti Bhavan in Lucknow is also playing the same role under the loving guidance of Swamiji.

Swami Nirviseshananda and Ma Gurupriya

Two main disciples of Swamiji are Swami Nirviseshananda (also known as Nutan Swamiji) and Ma Gurupriya. They have played a very significant role in the development of the Ashrama, and its activities have grown manifold under their care. Their scientific exposition of scriptures and approach to life has attracted persons from all walks of life to seek spiritual wisdom. Devotees feel equally blessed in their company and they are in themselves great exponents of spiritual knowledge.

Publications

Swamiji publishes an English monthly journal by the name of *Vicharasetu* (path of introspection) since 1968. Now it's Hindi and Malayalam versions are also being published. These journals have a wide circulation all over the world and serve as a bridge between Swamiji and his devotees. Though small in size, the journal is full of wisdom and effectively addresses the quest of readers. It also contains correspondence between Swamiji and his devotees, which makes the contents very practical. It also plays the role of a news journal for activities of the Ashrama and allied institutions.

Many books and CDs in English, Malayalam, Hindi, and Tamil have been brought out by the Ashrama. Notable among them are the following:

- Brahmavidya Abhyasa
- Vedantic Way of Living
- Quietitude of the Mind
- Science of Inner Redemption (2 Volumes)
- Divinizing Every Moment

About Swamiji and His Mission

- My Beloved Baba
- Essential Concepts in Bhagavad Gita (6 Volumes)
- Prabhaata Rashmih (3 Volumes)
- To the Householder
- Drops of Nectar from Srimad Bhaagavatam
- Genesis and Relevance of Temple-Worship
- In the Company of My Lord (by Ma Gurupriya)

These books present spiritual wisdom in a very rational and convincing manner and have benefitted millions of people.

Foundation for Restoration of National Value (FRNV)

Under the inspiration and guidance of Swamiji, the Foundation for Restoration of National Value (FRNV) was set up in June, 2008 to help promote national values in the Indian society. The advisory board of FRNV consists of Justice M. N. Venkatachaliah—former Chief Justice of India, Shri Ratan N. Tata—former Chairman Tata group, Dr. E. Sreedharan—the famous Metro-man, Shri N. Vittal—former Central Vigilance Commissioner, Smt. Vibha Parthasarathi—former Chairperson of National Commission for Women and Shri T. S. Krishnamurthy—former Chief Election Commissioner. With its secretariat at Delhi, FRNV is working to restore national values at a very fundamental level.

Anna Vastra Daana Satram

Swamiji strongly believes that one of the fundamentals of Dharmic life is "daana", which instantly rewards the giver and the receiver alike. At the same time, for the giver it is an inner enrichment and purification of wealth. In pursuance of this belief, Swamiji began annual *Anna–Vastra Daana Satram* in the year 1986 on a very small scale. This event has grown steadily, with large participation world over. In the year 2016 (31ˢᵗ year of *Daana Satram*), about 35,000 families were benefitted with a packet of rice, bed-sheet/saree and sweets. This is a mammoth task involving huge financial as well as managerial resources. But it is being carried out with increasing zeal and enthusiasm. Not only this, the event is being extended to other centres also. This is something which is unique in itself and instils inner expansion and elevation, strengthening the cultural bond and integrity.

Srimad Bhaagavata Tattva Sameeksha Satram

This large scale social event started in the year 2002 and is conducted at a specially created venue in Thrissur district in the month of December. Swamiji is a great exponent of wisdom of Srimad Bhaagavatam, which consists of 18,000 verses narrated to king Pareekshit, to redeem his mind from the clutches of doubt and suffering. The purpose of the event is to disseminate this wisdom to modern generation in order to change human life for the better. It is also a big event involving huge financial and managerial resources. The fact that the event is increasing in size and utility year after year, is an indication of the strong resolve of Swamiji.

Religio-Social Movements

Swamiji has also led various religio-social mass-movements in Kerala. It was in 1985, as a providential behest, that Swamiji went to the masses, to rid the society of some derogatory, illegal and cruel practices followed in the temples. Such practices, aided and abetted by vested interests, were perpetuated by the devotees for centuries, more out of fear of the divine than devotion. It was at the instance of righteous thinkers as well as Kerala's leading mass media that Swamiji and other Sanyasins took up the mission of eliminating such evil practices in the name of religion. It was the most important and unique religio-social movement Kerala ever saw.

Swamiji's entry into the field of religio-social reforms did shake the people of Kerala out of stupor. Even the insensitive minds were forced to reflect upon what is right and what is wrong and were compelled to take a clear stand. Many rational minds found reason and sense in Swamiji's thoughts and actions. But many held back due to fear of the unknown. They labelled him as "the controversial Swami". But most people did not care to know the unique spiritual attainment that inspired Swamiji to speak and act in the manner he did, with unswerving courage and confidence. His vision was clear: "The temples cannot remain as citadels of obsolete culture and inhuman practices. They must be the seat of loftier culture and civilization—a few steps ahead of the rest of the society." Eventually his resolve led to stoppage of such activities to a large extent, and today in Kerala Swamiji is accepted as a great socio-spiritual leader.

Swamiji also took up the formidable task of construction of the mammoth retention wall at Pandavagiri and the reconstruction of the Aykunnu Pandavagiri Devi Temple on the hilltop and completed it, working tirelessly with the labourers from morning to evening for years (Swamiji has mentioned about it in his letters given in this book). Initially, this task was considered to be impossible, but with divine grace it was successfully completed.

How could Swamiji have the courage and resolve to proceed with such mighty undertakings? The answer is, again, the same—*Atmana vindate veeryam*. The real source of courage is the "Self". The key to the multi dimensional *Loka-Sangraha* of Swamiji lies in his depth of Self-realization and the ascetic resignation. That makes him a non-doer and non-enjoyer, empowering him to do anything and everything, naturally, as does the Creator.

Contact: Narayanashrama Tapovanam
Venginissery, PO Paralam,
Thrissur Kerala-680563, India
Tel.: (0487)-2277963, 2278302, 2278363
E-mail: ashram@bhoomananda.org
Website: www.SwamiBhoomanandaTirtha.org

*****

23

Some Enlightening Write-ups of Swamiji

As a part of his wisdom dissemination pursuit, Swamiji has been constantly sending his write-ups through emails, Vichar-Sethu and other means. I have also been a recipient and beneficiary of them. Their number is large and can be compiled in many books. However, I have selected a few which influenced me most. I am including them in this book just to give a feel of this wisdom.

1. Rising above Afflictions

There are instances, where Deepavali, with its external illuminations, has a darkening note for some. There can no graver conflict or *dwandwa*. It is natural for human hearts to reminisce on their fond associations and memories. In fact, this is a facet not available to the other creatures on earth. Our mind has a dual function—of thinking about the present, which wrings concern for future; then to reflect on the past, which, in a way, is inseparable from the mind-processes. This course is what keeps mankind on their track. None can escape the influence of his past, nor can he be indifferent to the present and future.

This inescapability is what verily turns man a seeker and even Knower in the end. A parental heart thrives on its child-associations. When separation has been thrust on it, it cannot but awake now and them with its impact, however old and remote the instance may be, every time. This makes me also feel how deep the parent's pang with regard to a child is.

Many people question and wonder why grief or affliction should be the cause of spiritual seeking, in many cases. Nature's intention is to lead mankind to its own inner and hidden glories through joy and smiles. But she fails, because mankind gets lost in these, unable to generate any deeper insight. One shares his smiles and joys in the presence of others. It becomes a routine external sensory display. But when grief overtakes the mind, a shrinking or recession results. Mind turns inward. While joy takes the mind out, grief throws it inward. Naturally this inward process is the beginning of the inner pilgrimage, where the deity to be glimpsed is the Inner Lord Himself!

Affliction is thus very natural to gain proximity of the soul, because of the very nature of the emotion. But, unfortunately, most victims cry, weep, lament for a few days or months, and feel that time has healed their wounds.

Actually this should not be so. One has to be sincere in his loss, as he is in gains. Uddhava said he was unable to keep away from Krishna's lotus feet even for half a minute. He clung to his position. Krishna was equally hearty. Thus followed his last gospel, at the end of which Uddhava was able to leave Krishna before He left the world Himself. The unwilling servant got the wisdom and strength to keep away from the master, while the master was yet alive. Does not our mind then have the capacity to bridge any gap it suffers from?

God is the creator, sustainer and finally owner of everything in the world. He is the Lord to please Whom must be every one's aim. When He is pleased, he who strives to achieve His pleasure also gets fulfilled.

2. Resolving Conflicts

What is a conflict? It is the disparity the mind feels between what it wishes to see and what it sees, like what Arjuna encountered in Kurukshetra. In fact, conflicts help you discover true nature of the world, its inherent contradictory notes.

Beneath any conflict reigns its resolution too. Everything of the mind—be its reaction, urge or impulse—is like a wave in the sea. Even tsunamis subside and recede, leaving the earlier expanse and depth, unshakeable and stable. As the saying goes, after a storm there will be calm. Our mind is like a sentient sea. In it, all waves of conflicts and contradictions will subside. You will find a solution, or, the mind will dissolve them, to survive with greater majesty.

Let not your mind be small like a pond or a well. Not like a lake even. Let it be far greater. Think of it as having a sea or an ocean dimension. A number of waves and breakers rise in the sea. But the sea is not displaced by the waves and breakers. Even after a typhoon, the water will have to recede into the sea. You can raise your mind to still higher dimension—have a spatial mind.

Your mind produces thoughts. It generates emotions. Understand that the source is far greater than what it produces. Conflict is what the mind senses now. For the conflict, the same mind, which has got much deeper, vaster, and loftier dimensions, has a solution too. Look for that solution.

3. Our Infinite Dimension

The mind, intelligence and ego revolve around what we generally call the "Self" or the "Soul". I would like to put it this way: The body is at the gross level. Inside the gross body, employing the body is the mind. Still inward and superior is the intelligence. Still more so is the ego. Go beyond the ego and reach the Soul.

At the Soul level you will find that you have got a **"zero"** nature. There, no action or vibration ever takes place. No effect or affectation ever befalls there! It is a level into which none of the bodily, intelligential or egoistic effects reach. In the same manner, no action takes place in that level. We call it as "akartritva" and "abhoktritva" —a state of non-doer ship and non-enjoyer-ship.

Understand that such a level is there within you. It is already there. You do not have to acquire it. That is why, in spite of the gravest misfortunes and the greatest calamities and impacts, victims are able to go to sleep. When you recover from all the trouble and anxieties, it is your mind that recovers. And it does so only because of the Soul.

At the same time, the Soul is infinitely potent. All egoistic, intelligential, mental and physical activities are possible only in its presence. Understand that this Soul has a zero factor, and at the same time it is Infinite too! Whenever you want, you must be able to resort to its zero aspect or tap its infinite dimension. So, never become panicky. Do not be deluded thinking that to rescue you, some help should come from outside.

4. Way To Peace

Peace is one outcome of a good life, noble life, a spirited-religious philosophical life. Contentment is another outcome. Similarly you will find knowledge and knowledge fulfilment is another outcome.

Now, peace can be had in two ways. When you have a comfortable sleep you are peaceful, undisturbed, unaffected. Similarly when you are able to compose your mind in meditation or contemplation, the mind becomes free of thoughts and botheration and it can be led to peacefulness, for a time. The sleep lasts for long hours. This contemplative composure may last for a shorter spell.

As a contrast to this, there is a situation where you can have peace and that is what a good seeker should hunt, look for and enquire. That is when the mind becomes pure, and purer, and more and more qualities are imbued. This pursuit of purity, pursuit of qualities and goodness, directly brings peace to the mind, even while it is active and interactive. That is the final quest of all religions, philosophy, spirituality and yoga.

Whenever you feel anti-peace, understand that there is a cause behind it and look for it. Our shastras and tradition have identified the causes of lack of peace, and these identifications are as good as any other natural law or discovery in physics or chemistry. These laws and sequences of the mind operate constantly and these most ancient findings are true even today.

Two important qualities which will bring about and preserve peace are:

Having no expectation, no desire.

Sense of ego should not stand in the way of incorporating more and more excellences or virtuous notes, or eliminating the undesirable ones.

Throughout spirituality, you will find constant reference to ego and ego-effacement. This is one topic about which repetition is helpful—nay, necessary. Ahankara and mamata (ego and possessiveness)—both these are deep-rooted traits of the mind and they always victimize us.

Even with day-to-day seemingly insignificant events, the ego can manifest. With your own dear and near ones, you will find clashes of ego every now and then. Your children may not grow up exactly in the manner you want. When you want somebody to help you, the other person must have a helping nature. If he doesn't have it what can you do? Even Nature has not been able to introduce and consistently preserve good traits in human beings!

Take the Mahabharata: Did Krishna succeed in instilling a friendly attitude in Duryodhana? Could Bheeshma persuade his wicked grandson from perpetrating cruelty against his own brothers? Is there any law that the children will necessarily grow after the parents? When the opposite takes place, and it becomes a fact right in front of your eyes, why is it that your mind haunts you with these victimizing thoughts? Is it not ego? Is it not possessiveness?

You have to be very watchful about how the ego crops up. That will give you the clue as to how it has to be eliminated. Unless you are constantly on the path of self-sublimation, ego-effacement or self-effacement, I don't think you are going to have peace. Even a mustard measure of improvement, change of direction, change of attitude—can it not be had? That is all you need! So, personality improvement or refinement seems to be arduous. But it is not at all so. It is very easy and comfortable, once you know it well and have the will to do it. Unless ego and mamata are sublimated, you will not have even peace or happiness, why talk of enlightenment?

Spiritual life is a life where the seeker's mind is progressively harmonized, refined, enriched and empowered. It should become self-sufficient. When nothing is there, even with abject poverty, the mind should not grieve. Again, in the midst of prosperity, when things are plenty, the mind should not gloat over the condition. Neither praise nor riches nor recognition by others should affect the mind. You should be contented with whatever you get, be free of preference and prejudice, and also free of competition. Not be elated by getting what you like and not agitated to face what you dislike.

The mind must be able to live and outlive any situation. You must be able to generate your own contentment, poise, confidence and courage. Unless you are able to do this, we cannot call life as truly spiritual.

At the same time don't become fearful, diffident or obsessed by the impurities of the mind. It is enough if you are aware of them and if you are earnest about removing them.

5. Shraddha

Shraddha is the first and last word in any field of knowledge, both in gaining and expressing it. It should be even more so in the context of spiritual wisdom. If attentiveness is there, it will express itself in all the fields of one's life. The soul is present in everybody. Its presence alone activates the senses and initiates thoughts, emotions and knowledge. Without the soul neither the body can exist and function nor the mind, intelligence and ego, manifest. Yet, why is it that everyone senses the body but misses the soul? Even decades of efforts and austerity sometimes fail to clinch the search for the soul. Why?

It is sheer lack of attention to be sharp and focused on the goal. There is a general feeling that to be a spiritual person, seeker or Knower is to delight in unkempt hair, unclean dress and generally be careless about anything. Can there be a greater travesty?

Knowledge is noted for its sublime effects. It brings orderliness, rhythm, discipline and refinement at all levels. Only then can it make its votary worthy and effective in his interactions and achievements. In the name of knowledge how can one be unclean, disorderly and disorganized? Attention, *Shraddha* alone brings knowledge, retains it and employs it efficiently whenever and wherever needed.

It is true that spiritual seekers and votaries form an amazing assortment. That is because spirituality is amenable to one and all. So, all kinds of people, given to manifold habits and ways, also fill the spiritual arena. Let this be so.

But that is no reason for a sublime Knower to be shabby, haphazard and unrefined in the matter of living, moving, interacting, dressing and the like. *Janaka* sat on the throne and ruled *Mithila*, surrounded by knowledgeable ministers and advisors. He was yet a Knower.

What about Krishna, the Gita instructor? Can there be a better example? To think deeply, get at right conclusions, be able to express and give effect to them in an appealing and rational manner calls for considerable attention and application. So attention or *Shraddha* is something that cannot be ignored or sacrificed by the human at any time. It is all the more so in the case of seekers and Knowers.

6. Purpose of Spiritual Wisdom

Enumerating the divine qualities, Krishna gives a complete picture (in the 16th chapter of the Bhagvad Gita) of human traits and tendencies. The description naturally covers the devilish or destructive traits also. Krishna's list in this is longer and more detailed. Why should the evil tendencies be described at such length?

The *Saadhaka's* focus must always be on cultivating good and benevolent traits in himself. At the same time, he has to understand that the opposite qualities also go to constitute Nature and that in some, these traits and expressions may be more than in others. So, how to deal with evil and evil-mongers becomes a very crucial question.

It is possible that some destructive traits are either present in the seeker or are likely to entrap him any time. Moreover, the society he lives in is itself a blend of the two notes. He has to strive to safeguard against and win over the unwanted tendencies. So, he should be sufficiently poised to face the adverse notes and must go forward without getting unduly perturbed by them.

This means he has to make a provision in his mind for all kinds of individuals and groups around him. This is possible only through discretion and enlightenment, which alone have the power to contend and eliminate the *Aasuri* (non divine or evil) traits. The clarity and confidence instilled by this kind of spiritual enlightenment are ineffable. They alone can help the seeker go forward without hesitation.

The purpose of spiritual wisdom or enlightenment is to imbue the seeker with right perception and strengthen his mind and intelligence to be effective in any situation. In wisdom alone lie innate power, resolve and skill.

7. A Good Leader

If you want to an effective leader in any walk of life, you must be able to lead the mind and intelligence of others.

A good leader must first strive consistently to understand and strengthen his emotions, making them broader, deeper and loftier. Instead of being enmeshed in selfishness and mere personal and familial considerations, your mind should foster national and global fondness and concern. The intelligence should learn the culture of abiding by the norms of propriety, in whatever you think, speak or act. Only then you will have rational motivations and compulsions, appealing even to your rivals, not to speak of others. Hatred, intolerance and competition should be replaced by all-fold fondness, consideration and persuasion. Doubt or fear should not be allowed to hinder your thoughts and actions.

To administer the laws of the country and dispense with its resources is always a complex, challenging task, which calls for untold integrity, commitment and dedication. Single-handedly, with your mind alone for your support, you may sometimes have to contend with many individuals, groups, even a whole state or the Nation.

The strength of character, which wells forth from the notion of righteousness and propriety alone, will stand you in good stead ultimately. So the quality of the mind and intelligence is the only power and refuge for an Administrator. To do the great national task, you have been vested with the power, not just by a person or a department, but by the whole nation. Keep that in mind.

8. Be a Master of Your Life

When you see an object through the eyes, are the eyes seeing or do the eyes merely help in seeing? Where is this experience of seeing taking place? Where are the experiences stored? **My dear souls, interactions and perceptions proceed from the mind, they subsist on the mind, and they finally terminate in the mind.** So where is the focus and fulcrum of your life, my dear listeners? Is it not your mind? Are you conscious of this? Are you aware of it?

One thing is certain. There is definitely a need to study the mind. Normally, during the course of our education in the schools and colleges, this topic of mind is not explained. Many of you are parents. Have you ever told your children: "My dear boy, you are not the body. Your mind is immensely potent and great! Love your mind. Enrich it and beautify it!" Quite possibly, you have never spoken to your children about mind.

Why? Because, you yourselves have not made mind the focus of your life. This evaluation you have not taken up. With respect to the world and our interactions with it, what should be our assessment? Sri Krishna says (*Bhagavad-Gita* 3.42)

"*Senses are superior to the objects around. Mind reigns above the senses. And intelligence is still superior. But the Soul is still loftier. (It is the real identity of man.)*"

Krishna tells Arjuna that however great, imposing and huge the world may be, the senses are superior to the objects. With the small sensory organs, eyes, you can see a huge mountain. Who tells you that it is a mountain and it is huge? Whenever you interact with the world, or whenever you perceive the world, does the world perceive you? You are walking on the earth. You know that you are standing on it. But does the earth know that you are standing on it? When you see the sun rising in the morning, does the sun know that you are seeing it?

To employ the senses or not to employ them is your freedom and will. The senses by themselves cannot operate. Mind should command them to do so. Secondly, to see or not to see does not depend on the object. It depends upon you, the Subject. So, which is superior here? Are the senses superior to the objects or are the objects superior? Then, what about the mind which alone commands the senses? That mind is superior to the senses.

Let us go further in this line of thought. Krishna says: the intelligence is even superior to the mind. How? It can guide and influence the mind. A wrong thought can be identified and replaced by a good thought. In fact, all our discrimination is with regard to mind's feelings, responses and reactions. With this knowledge, how should we now look at the world and the various worldly phenomena? What should be our attitude, our response? What should be our aim?

Understand that all these are the thoughts and evaluations of our intelligence. So the intelligence is the one to show the direction to the mind. Still superior to the intelligence is the Soul that you refer to as "I".

It means you, the seer, are the most superior. But is this your assessment? I have heard people reporting: "Swamiji, we house-holders are insignificant creatures. I am a small man. I am nothing compared to the world." This is what everybody says. It is not so. Everything in you is superior to the world. You are the master of your life. Be not a slave to the world. This is the proclamation of spiritual wisdom.

9. The Right Perspective of Sukha-Dukha

Our purpose is to tackle the mind and redress the troubles and torments it generates. We also want to illumine the intelligence. Our mind is generally engaged in thinking about external objects and their impressions. So, let us give the mind and intelligence something loftier to constantly look into and enquire into.

When the mind and intelligence are occupied subjectively or spiritually like this, that occupation itself will carry us through and to that extent the external allurements will lose their importance. And ultimately you will find that your own mind, instead of depending upon external objects, starts generating its own internal comforts and delights.

Whether it is through interactions or not, it is the mind alone that generates delights and comforts. When the intelligence, too, gains ample clarity through knowledge, that knowledge-realization also will start giving you a lot of delight, so much so that external material object-based-delight will have lesser hold on you.

Now, let us apply the concepts of sat and asat to sukha and duhkha. Sukha as a substance or as an independent existence has no basis. It is not sat. Duhkha also has no basis of its own. Then how is it that they are manifesting?

See, no example can be perfect and complete. Examples can be helpful in understanding the concept. Think of fire. Fire certainly denotes an object. It reveals itself through two aspects: It generates heat and it brings about brilliance. Light and heat are the two properties or expressions of fire. Heat is a form of energy; so too is light. They are not themselves fire. But fire gives rise to these. We cannot have fire without giving rise to these two.

In the same manner *sukha* and *duhkha* are expressions or revelations which a third factor gives rise to. What is that third Factor in the presence of which *sukha* and *duhkha* are felt, and are expressed? If you go on probing and thinking in this manner you will find *sukha* or *duhkha* ceases to become important. Instead, that Third Substance which gives rise to *sukha* and *duhkha*—that causal factor or the Source—becomes a revealed entity. That entity is constant. It is the basis.

This Source reveals *sukha* and again after sometime it reveals *duhkha*. Both of them are alternately revealed by It. Now understand that this Third Factor, the Revealer can be sought, known and realized.

So, instead of running after *sukha*—which at best has only been deluding you—its presence becomes an occasion or a compulsion for you to search for and find out the source of *sukha*. In the same manner when *duhkha* manifests—leaving the feelings of *duhkha* aside—you must look for the source. And you will find the source of *sukha* and *duhkha* is the same. It remains intact and is present uniformly.

When you are able to shift your attention from the transitory *sukha-duhkha* to the ever present source, the problem of *sukha* and *duhkha* ceases. *Sukha* no longer deludes and attracts and *duhkha* no more afflicts and repels.

10. Mind Is the Seat of All Joy

Understand that the mind is the seat and source of all joy and fulfilment. Whether it is through the objects outside by interactions or not, the joy is always produced by the mind. If mind is the source of joy, keeping the resourceful mind within you, can you not become joyful? 'Yes', is the answer. Why is it that your mind is not becoming joyful? The reason is: It is disturbed by so many traits like egotism, possessiveness, greed, jealousy, intolerance, hatred and such other constrictions.

Now, having identified these, tell yourself, "I don't want all these constricting and harmful notes. I am interested in good elements." When the good thoughts come, welcome them and when the bad thoughts come, simply dissuade them. Dissuading means what? Do not love them. Do not linger with them. Simply say: "No!" That is all you are expected to do. When you dissuade the bad thoughts consistently for a period, those thoughts will become redundant. They will lose their currency. And they will not appear again and again.

But don't control them. Always meet them with an attitude of dissuasion. Your attitude should be: "I don't want these bad thoughts. I want to be good. I want to be glorious. I want to be happy. I want to be contented. I want to be joyous. And my joy will only come from within me. Whether other things are there or not, I want to be happy. And mind is the source of my happiness. When I get happiness, I don't need anything else." In this way, you have to think, rethink, evaluate, re-evaluate and grow to become refined.

11. The Three Gunas

The 14th chapter of Bhagavad Gita presents the philosophy of *guna-trayam*. Sri Krishna says that the entire nature is an aggregate of the three gunas—*sattva-guna, rajo-guna* and *tamo-guna*. The *sattva-guna* represents light, wisdom and happiness. *Rajas* represents passion, prejudice and the resultant activities. *Tamas* is a deterrent which produces ignorance, delusion, lethargy and sleep. You will find that these three gunas are spiritual constituents. They alone bring about all the changes, activity, actions, reactions, responses, everything—in the macro level and also in the micro level.

Being the constituents of nature, we won't be able to control them. Nevertheless, we have every opportunity and option to understand them properly and remain unaffected by them and transcend them. The best, the *sattva-guna*, try to manifest it more and more, increase its percentage. How can you increase the percentage of *sattva*? By pursing wisdom. Not only that, by looking for finer and deeper *sukha*, happiness.

The *sukha* that arises from the objects of the world by the interaction of the senses, by its very nature is transitory and leading to pain and discomfort. But if you look for *sukha* from your own mind and intelligence, that will be comparatively endearing. Rely more and more upon the inner comfort, inner enrichment and inner abundance, and *sattva-guna* will help you for it.

You can read the *shastras*, you can read Ramayana, Mahabharata, Sreemad Bhagavatam, and so many other spirituo-philosophical texts which are there. Spend some time in their association. Listen to spiritual discourses. These ideas get into your system and they get assimilated. The more and more they get assimilated, the *sattva* will increase and *rajas* and *tamas* will decrease. As a result, the mind will become subtler, keener. The intelligence will become more and more perceptive and there will be a greater play of knowledge and discretion in everything that you do.

When you ultimately outlive the three *gunas*, you understand that it is all *gunas* that play and you also understand the *gunâtita* Soul which gives you the freedom, peace and poise that you look for.

So, let us not be afraid of the world. Let us not be intimidated and frightened by the world. Your interactions with the world proceed from your mind and are subsisting on your mind. They also get completed, producing the effects and memory in your own mind. So in all our interactions with the world, the individual mind is the source, the sustenance and the terminus. What more do you want? Everything can be regulated, guided and also determined by your own mind.

To understand this and exercise this option for inner evolution and fulfilment is what human life is meant for.

12. Spiritual Seeker

A spiritual seeker will continuously be examining his thoughts, speech and actions. He is also watchful about the different types of perceptions and interactions he gets through knowledge organs, *jnaanendriyas*. Spiritual seeking is a continuous process, leading to greater and greater refinement and purification. In this, the seeker's intelligence plays a very important role.

"How is my mind? Am I thinking in the right way? Is there any rigidity in my thought process? Am I becoming too addicted to any of my pet notions? And because of the addictions, do I try to justify myself? Do I speak properly with straightforwardness? Or, is there any stealth or deception lurking in my words? What about the actions and activities that I perform—are they really impelled and persuaded by a clean and honest motive? Is my mind receiving proper inspiration and guidance from the intelligence? And what about the intelligence itself—is it getting illumined or enlightened?" In this way, the earnest seeker constantly examines himself.

When the intelligence receives the right input and you know what to do and what not to do, i.e., when the discrimination becomes sufficiently strong, it starts moulding the mind. The mind must receive it well, when the mind is so guided by the intelligence starts restraining the senses, the entire personality becomes sufficiently integrated and wholesome.

It is such an integrated, wholesome personality that spirituality aims at. The growth will be all-fold. In the bodily level, interactions with the world will go on harmoniously. In the oral level, you will start expressing what is in your mind without any corruption or stealth. In the mind level, you will always cherish good and auspicious thoughts. The wrong emotions are never promoted, but are discouraged through sublimation. The nobler emotions are nurtured, absorbed and preserved. At the intelligence level, contemplation will be upon the supreme reality, God, or on the extensive complex nature or on one's own inmost Self, the *Atma*.

*****